ROOKIE

By Richard Woodley

INSIDE THE WORLD OF BIG-TIME MARATHONING
TEAM
DEALER

ROOK

by Dwight Gooden

DOUBLEDAY & COMPANY, INC.

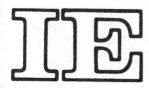

with Richard Woodley

GARDEN CITY, NEW YORK 1985

Library of Congress Cataloging in Publication Data
Gooden, Dwight.
Rookie.
1. Gooden, Dwight. 2. Baseball players—United States
—Biography. I. Woodley, Richard. II. Title.
GV865.G62A36   1985   796.357′092′4 [B]
ISBN 0-385-23093-1
Library of Congress Catalog Card Number 85–1590

To my mom and dad

Dwight Gooden's Rookie Year

In 1984 Dwight Gooden pitched 31 starts, 7 complete games, 218 innings, 3 shutouts, won 17 and lost 9, gave up 161 hits and 63 earned runs for an Earned Run Average of 2.60, walked 73, and struck out 276.

- Third highest win total in the National League, behind Joaquin Andujar (20) and Mario Soto (18).
- Second best ERA in the major leagues behind Alejandro Pena (2.48).
- Set the major league rookie strikeout record with 276.
- Set the major league record for ratio of strikeouts per nine innings with 11.39.
- Led the major leagues in strikeouts for the season—the first teenage rookie ever to do so.
- Led the major leagues by striking out 10 or more in 15 games.
- Led the major leagues with most strikeouts in a single game, 16 (tied with Mike Witt).
- Set a National League record by striking out 16 in 2 consecutive games for a total of 32.
- At 19, the youngest player ever chosen to play in the All-Star game.
- Second to Rick Sutcliffe in balloting for the National League Cy Young Award.
- 1984 National League Rookie of the Year.

ROOKIE

BOOK I

CHAPTER 1

April 1–April 12, 1984

I was sitting on the bench in the dugout watching the last few innings of our final spring training game at Al Lang Field in St. Petersburg. We were playing the Tigers. Right after the game, the Mets would break camp and fly to Cincinnati for the opening game of their 1984 season the next day, against the Reds. I wasn't on the roster. I was still a minor leaguer in the Mets' organization. I had been throwing the ball well during spring training and striking out quite a few batters, and the press had been giving me a good bit of attention, but I figured I would be going to Tidewater, the Mets' Triple-A farm team in Virginia. If I pitched well there, I figured maybe the Mets would bring me up to the big leagues after the All-Star break, or the next year. I was only nineteen years old, so I could be patient.

Davey Johnson, the new Mets manager, came over and sat down next to me. He put his arm around my shoulders. He said, "You made the team, in the four-man starting rotation." I said, "Yeah?" He said, "Yeah."

I couldn't say anything else. A feeling flowed through me, something I can't even explain. I didn't really know how to react. Suddenly I was on the Mets, a starting pitcher. Two years ago, I had been in Hillsborough High School in Tampa. I had been drafted from there by the Mets, spent a year in the Rookie League, a year in the Class A League, and pitched at the end of last year in the Triple-A championship series for Tidewater. All during spring training, I was sure I could pitch in the big leagues.

Right up until the moment Davey told me I was a Met, I was sure. But now I wasn't sure any more. Suddenly there was a little fear inside me. Was I really ready? Was I going to go up and embarrass myself or something like that? I didn't know how well I would compete on the major league level. Maybe it was too soon; maybe I wasn't good enough.

These things ran through my mind quickly while Davey sat there. Then he asked me if I had everything set and ready to go. I said, "Yeah." My bags were packed and I had brought them to the stadium, because I knew I would be going somewhere after the game—to Tidewater. That was what had happened the year before with my friend Darryl Strawberry. He had had a great spring, but the Mets had sent him to Tidewater for a while to get some at-bats and then brought him up later. I figured that's what they'd do with me. Strawberry had become Rookie of the Year.

But I was going straight up to the Mets to start the season in the big leagues, and I just hoped I could pitch well enough to stay there. Davey said, "Well, good luck, have a good season."

I had been dreaming about pitching in the big leagues since I was a little kid. Now I was in the dream, right there. I just kept telling myself that I would go up and throw like I had been throwing in spring training. I sat there telling myself that and waiting for the game to be over.

After the game I told my parents, who had come to say good-bye for wherever I was going. They hugged me. They seemed more excited than I did. My father used to tell me that when someday I went up to the big leagues, I would be playing on the same field with great players like Pete Rose and Mike Schmidt and all those I had watched on TV. That scared me. When he would tell me that, I would think that maybe I'd better go to college for a couple of years and come up to the big leagues when those guys were gone, because they were too big for me.

Now he teased me about that. He said, "Nobody's different, everybody dresses the same way." He asked me if I was scared. I said no, but inside I was. I just didn't want my parents to know.

I couldn't even tell my friends, because there wasn't time to make calls. The team took showers and got on a bus to the airport. An hour or so after our last spring training game, we were flying to Cincinnati. On Sunday, April 1, I was traveling for the first time with a big league team, the New York Mets.

I had never been in Cincinnati before. I had never been in any of the cities where the Mets would play while on the road, and we would be on the road for two weeks before going home to Shea Stadium. Much as I had dreamed about it, much as I had watched games on TV and seen big league players in spring training, I still didn't know how it would actually be to be a part of it. Everything was first class—plane, hotel. It was very different from the minor leagues. Right away when we got to Cincinnati I called my friends in Tampa to tell them where I was and what had happened. They were as excited as my parents. They said they looked forward to seeing me on TV—Tampa gets the cable broadcasts from Channel 9 in New York, which televises the Mets games—and that when the camera was on me I should wave and say hi.

I couldn't wait to get to the ballpark the next day. The trainers usually go in earliest to set up the training room to give players any treatments they may need. So I told Steve Garland, the head trainer, to call me when he was going over to the stadium. He called me about eight-thirty in the morning. I took a quick shower and got over there about nine. The game wasn't until two in the afternoon. The only people there in the locker room were Steve and Paul Grayner, the assistant trainer. Even the locker room was great, a lot bigger and nicer than in the minor leagues, totally different. It was what you dreamed about.

I went out into Riverfront Stadium. It was the biggest stadium I'd ever been in. I had seen it on TV, but it looked a whole lot bigger and nicer actually being there. The stadium completely surrounded the field, closed it in. I walked around on the field, all by myself, imagining what it was going to be like. The stands were empty except for a couple of ushers cleaning around the seats.

I walked out to the pitcher's mound and stood on it, just checking it out. It was kind of hard to believe I was actually there. It was like: What am I doing here? I'm only nineteen, and this is like a dream come true. I was real excited, real hyper, and when I'm that way I tend to talk very fast. But I wasn't talking to anybody but myself.

I was glad I wasn't pitching that day. I wouldn't pitch until our fourth game, in Houston, because Davey wanted me to be the fourth man in the rotation. I needed a couple of days to see what big league games are like when you're actually there on the field.

I couldn't wait for people to start getting there for the game to get started. It seemed like it took forever for game time to arrive.

Finally people started coming into the stadium, and it was time for batting practice. Mike Torrez, who was the real veteran of a pretty young pitching staff, would pitch that game against the Reds' star pitcher, Mario Soto. After I had done a little running and loosening up in the outfield, I was walking back toward the dugout when a little boy leaned out of the stands and asked me if he could have my autograph. He didn't know who I was. I said, "Sure," and I signed it. Some more kids came over and I signed autographs for them. It made me feel real big, signing autographs right there in the big leagues for my very first time.

Then some press people came over to talk to me. They said I was the youngest player in the National League and asked me how I felt about that. There wasn't much I could say except that it felt great, and age didn't matter —I would never use that as an excuse for anything. One of them said that a lot of rookie pitchers would be happy to have a .500 season. I said that would be great to have, but I wanted more. I said I'd like to go undefeated if I could. But that was just something to say. The fact was, I'd be happy to win half my games. I was happy just to *be* there.

It was the home opener for the Reds, and they had a big celebration on the field—fireworks, marching bands, horses. Even Johnny Bench was there on one of the horses. It was tremendous just watching all that, stuff you saw on TV and dreamed you'd see in person some day. And this was *on* TV. And there I was on the field.

But I didn't feel like I belonged there. I felt like a spectator. When the game started, and I was sitting on the bench watching, I felt detached, like I was up in the stands watching a big league game from there.

The crowd was a lot bigger than I'd seen—they announced about 46,000—because I was used to seeing minor league crowds. For some reason, I had sort of expected all the players to be giants. Even though I had seen a lot of them in spring training, still in my mind they were what I used to watch on TV, and I had thought maybe I'd be one of the smaller ones. But I was actually bigger than a whole lot of them. Logically, I should have known that, of course, because I am 6'3" and weigh 195 pounds. But I felt that big league players must be bigger.

Basically, I just sat there in the dugout watching everything that went on, mostly watching the hitters. I was a little intimidated by some of the hitters. The cuts they were taking seemed harder and better than what I had seen in the minor leagues. And a lot of the plays that were made in the field were just outstanding. Plus it seemed like every pitch Soto or Torrez threw must have been 95 or 100 miles per hour. That's how it looked to me. It was kind of hard to believe what was going on.

Some of our hitters were getting good wood on the ball—and these were guys I had struck out in intrasquad games during spring training, so that gave me an idea of what I could do, gave me some confidence. Strawberry hit a home run off Soto his first time at bat in the first inning. Just because he was my friend, and we had hung out together in spring training, made it unbelievably exciting seeing him hit that home run. I figured he was going to have another terrific season, and maybe the Mets would turn things around this year from being in last place the year before.

But Mike Torrez took some lumps, and Soto beat us, 8–1. For a little while after we lost, I was thinking about the past couple of years when the Mets were losing a lot, finishing last. I thought we might be the same old Mets, in for a long season.

Anyway, I was still kind of floating on air, even after the loss. After the game I went back to the hotel and called my parents, which is what I did after every game. I told my father that it had been great being at the game and how great things were in the big leagues. I had a hotel room to myself, and $42 a day meal money—which seemed like a lot compared to the $11 a day in the minor leagues. And the accommodations and travel were a lot better than the school buses we had in the minors. I called my friends, too, so my phone bill was something. But it was worth it, having people to talk to. I was still getting to know most of the players on the team.

A few of the players went out to clubs after the games. I went to a club with a couple of them, but I felt different. Everybody was older than I was. They all treated me fine and everything, but there wasn't anybody my age, and so I felt just different somehow. After a little while I left and went back to my room, where I was more comfortable.

The second game against the Reds, we won. Ron Darling, who was one of the group of young starters that included Walt Terrell and Tim Leary and me, shut out the Reds 2–0. He beat Bruce Berenyi, who looked like a real good pitcher to me. It was great to win, but for me it was still hard to realize that I was actually on the team, involved with what was going on. I felt as if I was still in the stands.

Then we took off for Houston. We flew in a chartered plane. Walt Terrell would pitch the first game there, I would pitch the second. Davey said he wanted me to make my first start in a controlled situation, in the Astrodome, where the temperature would be reliable and there wouldn't be any wind and the ball wouldn't carry so much. I was already getting pretty nervous about pitching my first game.

I was still looking forward to going to the ballpark every day, so I'd always be one of the first ones there. Houston was another new city for me, and I had never been inside a domed stadium before. Davey called a special workout to let the younger players get used to being inside a dome. The Astrodome was a strange place to think about playing baseball. There was the green artificial turf, and then way up above, maybe a couple of hundred feet, was the skylight. It felt more like you should be watching a basketball game or a boxing match in there.

The pitching mound surprised me because it was so high, which is good for fastball pitchers. And Houston had about the best there was in Nolan Ryan. That mound would also be good for me. The higher the mound, the better pitcher I am. It's like you're right on top of the hitters, and you can throw down.

Because I would be pitching the next game, it was my job to chart the pitches on the hitters for Walt Terrell—fill out the form where you mark down every pitch, what it was, what the batter did with it. Terrell was pitching well. He retired the first ten Astros in a row. Then I started thinking about it.

I started thinking: Well, this is the first game in Houston, and I pitch the second game. I hadn't thought much about it in Cincinnati because I just couldn't get over the fact that I was *there*. But now, while I was charting pitches in the dugout, it started taking effect on me.

We won the game, 8–1, with Terrell giving up only four hits, and George Foster, our left fielder, getting four hits, including a home run.

That game seemed to go by real fast—too fast, because I was pitching the next night and I didn't feel mentally prepared. I would have to face these same hitters tomorrow, and they would be hungry. And they would know I was a rookie in my first start. Plus the Mets were flying in my parents to see my first pitching start.

A reporter came over and told me that Nolan Ryan had

said he heard all about me and was anxious to see me pitch tomorrow. He wouldn't be pitching in the series, but he wanted to watch me. The reporter asked me how I felt about that. Nolan Ryan has been a star pitcher for 15 years or something like that, and had more strikeouts than anybody else in the history of baseball, and he was somebody I idolized. I used to pretend I was him back in Little League. I'd never seen him pitch except on TV. Hearing that he wanted to see *me* pitch—before I had even pitched once in the big leagues—well, that was an honor.

That night, I couldn't help thinking about the game. I couldn't really sleep. I was thinking: Tomorrow's my day. I gotta pitch. What might happen? How will I react if they hit me? Were they all just going to hit everything I threw out there? How was I going to handle myself in front of a bigger crowd than I'd ever pitched in front of before?

Because of my success in the last couple of years in the minors, a lot had been written about me lately, and I felt the pressure of it. The year before, when I was eighteen, I had a record of 19–4 with Lynchburg in the Class A Carolina League. At one stretch I won 15 straight and went 46 consecutive innings without allowing an earned run. I ended up with a 2.50 ERA and struck out 300 batters in 191 innings, which was a record for that league. Then at the end of the season the Mets brought me up to Tidewater to help them win the Triple-A championship and world series, and I won two out of three. *Baseball America* named me Minor League Player of the Year.

So this year at spring training the press wrote a lot about me being some kind of phenomenon or something, destined to be a star with the Mets. They wrote about my pitches and my control and my competitiveness, and all kinds of stuff. That was all nice publicity to

have, and I was proud of what I had accomplished so far.
But I was in the big leagues sooner than I or anybody else
had figured I would be. And now I was about to pitch my
first big league game. I sure hoped I wouldn't embarrass
myself or anybody else. I hoped I wouldn't let Davey
Johnson down, or the team, or my parents, or my friends.
I had never been so nervous in my life about throwing a
baseball.

I tried to just think about pitching the best way I knew
how and hoped that things would go my way.

I got up earlier than usual and ate breakfast. Already
the time was dragging. By noon it seemed like a whole
day had gone by. The game wasn't until seven-thirty.
The team bus was scheduled to leave the hotel around
five o'clock. I couldn't wait for the bus. I was too anxious
to get to the Astrodome, so I decided to walk. It was
about a mile and a half. I was really tense about the game.
So I walked by myself, thinking about the game and
trying to relax.

I got to the stadium at about two-thirty. A couple of
players were there getting treatments in the training
room. I just paced around and got dressed slowly, trying
to make the time pass. To calm my nerves, I kept trying
to tell myself just to do the things that got me here, be
myself, and go out and have fun.

Finally we went out on the field for batting practice.
There were already people in the stands. I didn't feel like
myself. I felt like a totally different person when I walked
out on the field in a Mets uniform. I swung the bat a few
times in the batting cage and hit a couple balls pretty
good. I loosened up a little. And before I knew it I was in
the bullpen, throwing to warm up. I was chewing on a
wad of gum and feeling good and staying calm. I was
throwing pretty hard. Lots of times, when I'm nervous I

have a little more velocity on my fastball. So I guess I was trying to stay calm, but I was hyper.

Mel Stottlemyre, our pitching coach, was watching me warm up in the bullpen and asked me how I felt. I said, "Great." He said, "Just throw the ball like you did in spring training." I said, "Okay." But that was easier to say than to do. This was a real game, and I was going to be watched by all these people in the Astrodome, and on television. People in New York would be watching, and Tampa. And I knew my parents were sitting over there by our dugout someplace.

I was throwing the ball okay in the bullpen, but when I went back to the dugout for the game to start, I began to get real anxious. We hit first, and I wanted us to make three outs fast. I wanted to get out there on the mound and see how it'd be. I wanted to get on with it, see how I could pitch in the major leagues. So in spite of myself, I was sitting in the dugout just wanting our hitters to hurry up and make three outs right away so I could get out there.

The Astros' pitcher, Bob Knepper, was throwing the ball pretty well. He got Ron Gardenhire, our second baseman. But then shortstop Jose Oquendo got a hit. Finally Knepper put down two of our best hitters, first baseman Keith Hernandez and left fielder George Foster. It was time for me to pitch in the big leagues.

Davey had told me to start off slow and just give him five good innings. I walked out to the mound slowly, taking my time, trying to be relaxed. The first couple of warm-up pitches I threw to catcher Mike Fitzgerald, I wasn't really thinking about what I had to do to get hitters out. First of all, I didn't want my first warm-up pitch to get away from me and go into the stands. The first pitches I was just throwing, going through the motions. I wasn't loose. I was stiff and couldn't throw like I should. I was thinking that it was good to be pitching in a domed stadium because the ball wouldn't carry so much and that I was pitching off a high mound, which is good for a fastball pitcher. But I wasn't thinking about my pitches.

When the umpire said, "Play ball!" it really hit me. I had to walk off the mound and get myself together. I told myself: Just throw strikes and let everything else take its own course. The first thing I was thinking about was that I didn't want to walk anybody.

The first hitter I faced in the big leagues was Bill Doran, their second baseman. I had pitched to quite a few major leaguers in spring training, but I had never faced Doran. I didn't know much at all about him. I had just skimmed over the previous night's pitching chart. He was hitting left-handed.

I figured that the first few Astro hitters might be taking my first pitches, to see how I'd throw my first time out. So I was going to go right at them. Mike Fitzgerald would call a majority of fastballs, and we would start off every hitter with a fastball.

My first fastball was a little outside and Doran took it for a ball. My second fastball, he hit a grounder to Gardenhire at second for the first out. Then Terry Puhl grounded out to second also. I took a deep breath. They weren't taking a lot of pitches. They were coming right at me, swinging at everything. I had thought I was throwing hard because, as I say, usually I will overthrow if I'm nervous, and I was really nervous. But the first two hitters had pulled my fastball. I had to concentrate more.

I got the count to 2–2 on Dickie Thon, the shortstop, a good hitter. He fouled one off over by our dugout, and when I glanced over I saw my parents for the first time. I tried to pretend they weren't there. I had told them not to say anything to me or draw my attention until the game was over. I threw Thon a hard fastball. I meant to go down the middle with it, but I overthrew and got it up. He swung and missed. My first major league strikeout. I knew at least I could throw the ball by somebody.

But when I was walking off the mound, I couldn't believe I had struck him out, especially on a high fastball. People had told me before that you might get away with a high fastball in the minor leagues, but in the big leagues you aren't going to. But this time I got away with it.

I sort of cut my eyes up at my parents, hoping they weren't looking at me while I was looking at them. But they were watching everything I did.

When I got to the dugout, my teammates were happy with the way the first inning went, and so was I. The most important thing was that nobody got on base, so I was more relaxed and ready for the next inning.

In the top of the second, Strawberry belted a home run over the center field fence. We all jumped up to greet him when he came in and gave him high fives. He asked me, "Is that enough?" I said, "No, I'll take all I can get." But at least that gave me a one-run cushion.

I had a little more confidence going out there in the second inning. The first inning I had had some control problems, but they were swinging at a lot of high fastballs out of the strike zone, pitches I thought they would be taking. In the second, left fielder Jose Cruz, their hitter I was most afraid of, grounded out to short. He was late on the fastball, so I knew it was coming in good. I started mixing in some curveballs when I got ahead in the count. I struck out the next two hitters, Jerry Mumphrey and Ray Knight.

I had retired the first six batters I faced, and between innings I started thinking I really could pitch in the big leagues. Getting a lot of strikeouts never crossed my mind. I didn't think I could be a strikeout pitcher in the major leagues. I was just happy to be getting the outs.

In the third, I gave up my first walk, to Denny Walling, and then my first big league single to catcher Alan Ashby. I had heard about Ashby, since he is the catcher for Nolan Ryan. He got kind of a cheap hit to the opposite field, on a fastball. At first I thought: Uh-oh, now they've seen me throw to a few hitters, maybe I'm in trouble. Oquendo tossed me the ball and just said, "Okay, now, next batter down."

So I said to myself: Well, that's a hit, the first hit. Now I have to get the next batter to hit a ground ball for a double play or something, because there were two runners and no outs. I struck out Knepper, the pitcher, and Doran, then got Puhl on a fly ball to end the inning.

The team was really behind me, not just encouraging me when I was on the mound, but getting some hits. In the fourth, Hernandez singled, Foster doubled, and center fielder Mookie Wilson scored them both with a double. I had a 3–0 lead.

I got through the fourth without problems, but in the fifth I gave up my first run on a couple of hits and a stolen base by Walling—I knew stolen bases were going to be a problem for me, because I hadn't held runners on too well in the minors either. Doran singled to score the first run off me.

After the fifth, Davey took me out. He said I had given him the five good innings he wanted—five was the most I had pitched in spring training—and had thrown 81 pitches, which was enough for the first time out. I had had some small problems in spring training with my lower back and a split fingernail, and he didn't want those aggravated. He wanted to bring me along slowly and give me time to learn the league and the hitters. He said he was satisfied. I probably could have gone six innings. But after the fifth I was getting tired. It was enough.

But I didn't go in and take a shower. I stayed on the bench to watch the rest of the game. I left with a 3–1 lead, and I wanted to see if I would get the win. Dick Tidrow had relieved me, and they loaded the bases on him. Ray Knight hit a long ball that looked like it might be a grand slam. I watched it go and thought my win was going with it. But it went foul.

The Astros got a run, but Doug Sisk and Jesse Orosco shut them out the last three, and I had my first major league win, 3–2.

I had pitched only five innings, but I felt as drained as if I had pitched a whole game. I was overthrowing a lot, that's why a lot of my pitches were up. I was told that they had clocked my fastball in the beginning at 91 miles per hour, and the top speed later at 94. But as far as my pitches being up, our hitters were telling me that wasn't so bad. When the hitters have two strikes on them, it's good to throw up and in, because when you throw as hard as I do, a fastball high and tight ties a hitter up.

I was satisfied with my first time out—five innings, three hits, one run, five strikeouts. But the main thing was getting that first win.

After that, I was looking forward to somebody asking me for my autograph. I had given some autographs in Cincinnati, but nobody asked for *me,* personally. Next day at the Astrodome I was walking to the dugout when somebody called from the stands, "Hey, Gooden!" I turned. I thought maybe it was somebody I knew. It was two ladies near the dugout. They said they wanted my autograph, and they held out a pencil and paper. I signed it. One of them said, "You pitched a great game yesterday." That was the first time somebody had asked for me by name. It made me feel like I was starting to belong.

We won the game that day too, with Mike Torrez pitching six innings of shutout ball before giving up a run against Joe Niekro, and Tim Leary getting the win in relief when the Mets scored two in the eighth.

But the thing that did not make anybody feel good was Dickie Thon getting hit by a Torrez pitch in the third. Even though I didn't know him, Thon was the first player I had struck out in the game the day before, so I would always remember him for that reason. But he was also known as a good, clean ballplayer, and nobody wanted him hurt. At first I thought he was just hit in the helmet and would be okay. But he fell and rolled over and didn't move. They called an ambulance and took him away. When I found out he had been hit in the eye and couldn't play any more that year, I felt bad.

But I was glad for Torrez, the way he had pitched. I knew he had been a little shaky last year, and then had lost his first start against Cincinnati this year. Plus the fact that he was thirty-seven maybe made him worry a little about his position with the Mets. Being such a veteran pitcher, he was able to be very helpful to me and the other young pitchers, telling us how to pitch to certain hitters he knew. So I was glad he had a good game. That gave us a sweep of the Astros.

Then we went to Atlanta and took two games from the Braves, 4–2 and 6–1. Ron Darling gave six strong innings in the first game, and Craig Swan got the win in relief. Strawberry hit another home run—his third in six games—and Hubie Brooks, our third baseman, hit his first. In the second game, Walt Terrell gave up only five hits.

Strawberry was getting lots of hits, hitting with power, driving in runs. I had heard so much about what he could do, and the way he was going I thought this would be the year he would show everything. Not only him, but the team—I thought we were on our way to the World Series.

We had won six in a row since our opening loss to Cincinnati, the team's longest winning streak since 1979, and it was the best start since the team was founded in 1962—two years before I was born.

Actually, I wasn't aware that this was the fastest start in Mets history until some reporters brought it up. It was a good start, but it wasn't the kind of start you figure would be a record. I was aware, though, that the Mets had finished last in the National League the last two years.

I figured that the Mets' losing so much had helped my chances of getting to the top quicker. If I had been in the Phillies' organization when they were winning, or the Yankees', I wouldn't have moved to the majors so fast, let alone get into the starting rotation.

While I was coming up, I knew we had a lot of great players in the minor leagues, and I figured in a couple of years that would have a big effect on the Mets. But already in spring training, I thought the team was going to change a lot sooner. Keith Hernandez had come over from the Cardinals the year before, and he was one of the best fielders and hitters in the game. And Strawberry had just come up last year. We had almost a totally different pitching staff also. Ron Darling and Walt Terrell had come up from Tidewater last year, and it looked like they were going to be great pitchers.

I didn't think I'd make such a big contribution. Just by watching Terrell and Darling, and then Torrez, who'd been around for a while—just by watching them on TV, I thought I might be the worst pitcher on the staff. If I finished .500, that'd be really outstanding for me. In the beginning, my main object was just to try and do well enough not to get sent back down to Tidewater. On the other hand, I didn't want them to look at me and say, "You're the one we're worried about." So when I came up, I made up my mind that if they did their jobs, I'd be okay.

By now the ERA for all our pitchers together was 2.03, lowest in the league. We were leading the National League East. Things were really starting to change for the Mets. I was looking forward to my next start, against the Cubs in Chicago, our last stop before going home to Shea Stadium for the first time this season.

CHAPTER 2

1970–1984

Baseball has been the main thing for me for as long as I can remember. My father, who is retired from a chemical company because of arthritis, used to play some semipro ball and coached a semipro team. I followed him around. When I was about six, he took me over to Lakeland to watch the Tigers in a spring training game. I saw Al Kaline hit a couple of home runs. So Kaline was my idol. I wanted to play the outfield and hit home runs in the big leagues like Al Kaline.

When I was seven, I joined the Belmar Heights Little League, the minor league part of it for the youngest kids. But I was afraid to play in front of my parents, so I quit. They were never hard on me or critical or anything. I was just small and shy. The next year I went back, and I pitched. I wasn't afraid to play in front of my parents any more, but the team was so bad that I was humiliated. Everything was errors, and we would get beaten by 10 or 15 runs. The team was in last place, 3–16 or something like that. I hated the idea of losing so much that I would cry. So I ended up quitting again. My father asked me why I quit, and I said because they're a lousy team. I'd be out there hustling and the other kids would mess up. I couldn't stand being part of that.

My father said it wasn't their fault that they couldn't play any better, and they were doing the best they could. He said he would let me quit this one more time, but that if I quit again I couldn't play baseball any more.

Next time in Little League, I was ten. I started out in the minors, but the coach of my team, the Reds, played for my daddy's semipro team, so he had watched me a lot and he knew that I could play pretty well. He moved me up to the majors, which is for eleven- and twelve-year-old kids, and he put me at third base. I was one of the smallest kids there. There were some big kids who could really throw. I went 0 for 5 my first times up, and struck out three times. I was scared. There was one pitcher, Albert Everett, who could throw really hard. In one game, he hit a batter in the eye. I was scared to bat against him. So I went to a director of the league and told him I wanted to go back down to the minors because I was afraid to play in the majors with the bigger kids.

But he thought I could make it, and he urged me to stay. I ended up as the starting third baseman. We won the championship and the team went to the 1975 Little League World Series in Williamsport, Pennsylvania. I couldn't play in the world series because you had to be at least eleven years old. Our team lost to Taiwan.

By the time I was eleven, I was starting to grow and get a lot taller. Now I was one of the bigger players. And I was getting pretty good with the bat and the glove. My confidence was growing. But I wasn't very patient with the other players. Where once I had always been wanting to quit, now I was starting to yell at players when they made mistakes. At a practice one time somebody forgot to bring a ball, so we were just standing around. I started thinking about how I acted, yelling at people. I remembered what my father had said, how everybody couldn't be as good as everybody else and that they were trying their best. I felt guilty about it. I'm a quiet person, usually, and don't say too much about what's bothering me. But when we were standing around there, I thought: This is the right time to say what's on my mind. So I said, "I'm sorry for the way I act sometimes." They laughed and teased me and said that I thought I was too good, as if they didn't accept it. But that was just their way of reacting out loud. I knew they accepted what I said. And things were good with the team and me after that.

I learned from that experience. I guess something just changed me overnight, about being tolerant of other players who make mistakes. I won't be the type to get on anybody again, even if I'm a star.

I was developing a pretty good arm, throwing from third base, so when I was twelve I started pitching again. I pitched a perfect game. We were playing Progress Village, our rival, and the stands were full. I pitched to 18 batters and struck out 16. One guy bunted back to me and I threw him out; another guy bunted to first base for the out. I also hit two home runs that game. We won, 7–0. It was the most exciting moment I had ever had—my biggest thrill right up to when I got drafted by the Mets. I don't think I went to sleep at all that night, just thinking about what I had done.

Our high school, Hillsborough, was loaded with pitching talent when I started there. They had my old rival, Al Everett, who was later drafted by the Twins, Vance Lovelace, who was a first-round pick of the Cubs in 1981, and Floyd Youmans, who was a little older than I and a close friend. When I was a sophomore, I played in the summer Senior League, which is an older version of Little League, for kids fourteen to fifteen. That year my Senior League went to the world championships in Gary, Indiana. That was the first time I ever flew in an airplane. I didn't pitch then, I played shortstop against Taiwan. Taiwan usually wins everything. Their players look a lot older and a lot bigger. They're supposed to be the same age we are, and they say the reason they play so well is that they play year round and have a school for baseball. But you don't get to be six feet tall when you're only fourteen just by playing year round. In any case, we lost to Taiwan, just the way we did in Little League.

I was still having a little trouble controlling my temper sometimes. I didn't yell at other players, but I got angry. In one game, things just weren't going my way at all. We were giving up hits, walks, errors. And this was against one of the worst teams in the league. After one inning I came back to the dugout, slammed down my glove, and banged my arm into the wall. I sprained my wrist, and that kept me out for about a week. Sometimes I used to get real upset when we'd lose or I'd do something wrong, and I'd throw my glove over the fence or fling a bat or helmet. I don't do that any more. Like not yelling at other players, I guess it was just an overnight thing—I woke up one morning and everything was changed. I had to stop doing stupid stuff. I got a lot of help from my family on that. When people write about my being poised, it's really just a matter of not doing stupid things that mess up your game or your concentration.

I was born on November 16, 1964, in Tampa, Florida. I have three older brothers and two older sisters—all 10 to 18 years old. My brothers, James, Danny, and Charles, were from my father's first marriage, so they were always away.

We never had a lot of money, but we were okay. We lived in a sort of working-class black neighborhood in

East Tampa, in a one-story, three-bedroom house pretty much like the other houses in the neighborhood.

When I was ten or eleven, my friends and I used to make a little spending money in the summer doing things like mowing lawns, cleaning up yards, or selling fruit. We had a big avocado tree in the back yard, and when the fruit fell off the tree we used to gather it up, load it into a buggy, go to the grocery store, and sit right outside the door there and sell it. Nobody would ever bother us about it. We'd sell the avocados for a quarter or 30 cents apiece, and come home with maybe $30. We could sell four or five buggy loads during the season. Then sometimes when people were coming out with their groceries, we'd ask them if they needed any help, and we'd carry the bags of groceries for them and they'd give us a tip.

Mainly, though, in the summer we used to play baseball or football, or go to swimming pools, or take bike rides around the parks. My mom—she's a nurse's aide—wanted me to work at a regular summer job. I wanted to work sometimes. When Wendy's first started in business, I brought home a couple of job applications. But my father said I didn't have time for a full-time job. He cared mostly about sports. He wanted me to be an athlete. He told me to go easy, just worry about baseball.

Next to baseball, I really liked football and basketball. But once when I was playing football (I was about eleven), somebody stepped on my wrist and broke it. That was enough football. Basketball, though, I kept playing. I love basketball. Every Sunday we'd play, either in the park or over in the gym. That was one of my better sports, and we could play all day long on Sundays.

But baseball was always my first love. I took it seriously. I have a nephew, Gary Sheffield, who's about four years younger than I. He was staying with us for a while, when I was about ten or twelve, and he was more like a brother. He liked baseball, but not as much as I did. I figured, if I like baseball a lot, he's got to like it a lot too. I forced him into playing. I'd really get on him. When I'd get up early in the morning, I'd wake him up also. I would have eaten breakfast by then. He hadn't eaten or showered or anything, but I'd wake him up and make him go out and play baseball, just the two of us.

I'd pitch to him, he'd pitch to me. I made him work. If I hit the ball down the street, he'd have to go get it. If he hit the ball down the street, he still had to go get it. I'd end up fighting him. Lots of times he'd cry and want to quit. He'd go in and tell my mom that I beat him up because he wouldn't throw the ball the way he was supposed to. But then he'd come back out and play. I'd make him play. I wasn't very nice about it.

Now, though, he's glad I did that. He told me last year that all that had made him a better player and a better person. Now he likes the game a lot. He's a junior at Hillsborough High. I don't know how much I helped him, but last year he struck out 21 batters in a game. That's better than I ever did. He's going to be a good ballplayer.

As far as personality, in our family I probably most resemble my father, in that we're both kind of quiet. He helped me become a ballplayer and learn to take the good with the bad, learn from your mistakes, and come back the next day. My mom helped me a lot with my attitude problems and temper by talking to me about how people are watching you all the time and how stupid you make yourself look when you let your temper go. My sisters, Mercedes and Betty, helped me out a lot too. Betty, my youngest sister, who's thirty-five now, was like another mom. I could go to her with anything.

I guess I learn pretty well from making one mistake

and doing better next time. Usually I don't come back and make the same mistake over again. Even today, if things start going a little bad, I use that experience when I got mad and slammed my wrist into the wall and sprained it—it reminds me that I just made myself look stupid and messed myself up. If things start going wrong for you, you've got to ask yourself: Why do something stupid? Why get mad? Forget about it. Blank it out of your mind and get the next hitter. Some good players have come out of Tampa high schools. Lou Piniella went to Jesuit. Wade Boggs went to Plant, which was one of the teams Hillsborough played. Steve Garvey went to our rival, Chamberlain. Mike Heath went to Hillsborough.

The Hillsborough baseball coach, Billy Reed, has been around a long time and he really knows how to develop players. He used to do some scouting for the Cincinnati Reds, who have their spring training camp in Tampa, and he brought pro players around to school.

Billy Reed was a tough coach, probably the toughest I've had. He got everything out of you he could, forced you to use all your talent. To him, baseball was more than just getting out there and having fun, it was really working at it. He had played ball himself, besides scouting, so he knew what to do. Hillsborough has been as successful as it has for so many years because he is so tough and knowledgeable. He didn't care if you liked him or not, as long as you did what he said and did it the right way.

He was very good for me, especially in my senior year. I thought I was the best player on the team, and maybe I wouldn't have worked so hard if he'd have let me coast. But Coach Reed never let me rest on how good I was or thought I was. He doesn't care if you go undefeated or hit 30 home runs or whatever, he's going to treat you like everybody else, and he never let me feel irreplaceable. He made me work hard. He helped me in more than just pitching. He helped me in hitting and fielding different positions. He made me a better player without ever knocking down my confidence.

In my junior year, the top pitcher on our staff was a senior, Vance Lovelace, who is now in Double-A ball with the Dodgers. And ahead of me as a junior pitcher was Floyd Youmans, who was also a junior. So that year I was more of a reliever. I was also playing third base and the outfield. I liked third base because there was a lot of action and I could play every day, and I was a good hitter.

I was also learning how to pitch. Coach Reed showed me different ways to grip my fastball to give it better movement, and how to get more rotation over the top on the curve. I pitched a game in the Easter tournament, a one-hitter. I faced the minimum of 21 batters in the 7-inning game. The guy that got a single was thrown out trying to steal. I walked one guy and he got thrown out trying to steal also. I was named Most Valuable Player of the tournament. As a junior pitcher, I went 7–0, with a 0.76 ERA.

Then in the summer I played in what is called the Big League, similar to American Legion baseball. I was hitting well and striking out a lot of batters. People started giving me the nickname Doc, like Dr. J, Julius Erving, who was my idol as a basketball player. When I was going well with my fastball, people used to yell out to me, "Operate on him, Doc!" People have called me that ever since.

The Pittsburgh Pirates sent some scouts out to look at me. They timed me in running sprints. They didn't want me as a pitcher. They were looking at me as a third baseman or outfielder, because I swung the bat pretty well.

In my senior year, Floyd Youmans moved to California. That left me as the only veteran pitcher, the top pitcher on the staff. Actually we had only about three or four seniors left on the team, so it was a rebuilding year, and our team was not outstanding.

I got a chance to pitch in almost every game, and I did play in every game, even when I didn't pitch. We played Tuesday, Friday, and Saturday, with a lot of night games. Whether I was the starting pitcher on Tuesday depended upon the team we were playing. If we were playing a good team, I would start. Then if we were winning by three or four runs, I'd come out and play third or short or the outfield. Sometimes, if scouts were there, Coach Reed would let me stay in and pitch even with a big lead. On Friday, if the game was close I'd pitch maybe the last couple of innings. Then I'd start Saturday's game. Sometimes when I was playing third, and he thought there was a good chance I might pitch later in the game, he'd save my arm by putting me in right field. But I was always in the game, so I was hitting all the time.

In my senior year, I hit .340, and I loved to hit. But by then I was mainly a pitcher, and I was never sorry about changing. I thought that a pitcher or catcher had a better chance of making it to the big leagues, and that's what I was thinking about. My pitching record that year was not all that great—7–4. I lost games by scores like 2–1. There were lots of errors. The only time I really got mad that year was because of errors.

In one game the other team got an unearned run off me in the third inning by three errors. One third baseman fielded a ground ball and threw over first, clear into the stands, letting the batter go to second. Then a grounder went through the second baseman's legs, and the guy scored. I hit a home run in the fourth to tie it up. We went into the bottom of the seventh tied, 1–1. The leadoff batter hit a ground ball to short that went through the shortstop's legs. The left fielder charged it, and it went through his legs too, all the way to the wall. The throw came in and went over the cutoff man's head. The next throw went over the catcher's head. The batter went all the way around to score. It was like the Bad News Bears. After pitching a game like that, and my hitting a home run for our only run, to lose by two unearned runs was unbelievable. I went into the dugout swearing and slammed my glove down, because I just couldn't believe what had happened.

Still, for the year I had an ERA of 0.75, and 135 strike-outs in 74 innings. A lot of scouts were coming around to the high school games, and they would give you information cards to fill out, showing whether you were planning to attend college or if you would sign to play pro ball.

So I figured I would be drafted. I thought I might go to the Reds, Cubs, or California Angels, because a lot of their scouts were coming to the house and talking to me and giving me eye tests. They had something like a camera that you looked into and saw numbers, and they asked you what you saw, and then they changed to different colors. They also used to come to my high school and take me out of class and bring me to the library and give me eye tests and ask me questions.

At that time, my dream was to go to the Reds, because they had invited me to their tryout camps in my junior and senior years, just to throw to other guys trying out. So I was a Cincinnati Reds fan. In their big winning years I always dreamed about playing with guys like George Foster, Pete Rose, Joe Morgan, Ken Griffey, Johnny Bench—guys I had seen on TV or at spring training games in Tampa.

Next to the Reds I liked the Pirates. I had never seen the Pirates other than on TV. But once I met Willie

Stargell. He was there when our Little League team went to the Little League World Series—the time I couldn't play because I was only ten. I got to meet him and talk to him. So I fell in love with the Pirates; that was my second-favorite team.

But of course I would have been happy to be drafted by any team. And while I figured I would be drafted, I never figured I would be a high pick because of my mediocre 7–4 record that last year in high school.

If the draft didn't work out, I could go to college. I wasn't a great student in high school. I got mainly C's. But I got quite a few letters from colleges saying they were interested in me and asking if I would be interested in attending. They all said they would give me a scholarship.

About three weeks before our baseball season was over, the University of Miami said they would get me an apartment. The last couple of years they had kind of fallen down in baseball, but from about 1978 to 1981 they were great. I had already decided that if I got drafted in the first five rounds, I would sign to play pro ball. But if nobody came up with a decent deal for me, I would go to college. And if I went to school, Miami is where I decided I would go, to play baseball for the Miami Hurricanes. So I replied to them that I was interested.

My mom wanted me to go to college. She never really did understand about baseball, about it being a profession for me. But I guess she realized that the thing I really wanted to do was play pro ball. I was giving college some serious thought, but deep down pro ball was what I wanted. I never really liked school all that much, the homework and getting up early in the morning. So I was hoping I'd get drafted high enough. If that hadn't happened, I would still be in school now.

After the high school season, my arm was a little tired
—I had thrown a lot of pitches. The draft didn't come
until June 7, so I went into that summer big league again.
Since the coach figured I was going to get drafted as a
pitcher, he mainly played me at third base and in the
outfield to save my arm. A couple of games, though, like
when the Angels' scouts came over and wanted to see me
pitch, he did let me pitch a few innings.

The day before the draft, a reporter at the Tampa
Tribune who used to do a lot of write-ups on me called me
up and asked me if I wanted to come down and watch the
draft come across on the computer. I said that would be
great, and one of my friends and I went down there the
next day. We got there about an hour before the draft
started. They served us doughnuts and oranges, and we
looked through a lot of papers and pictures they had,
waiting for the draft to start.

Then when it started we watched the names come
across the screen. It showed first round draft and the
name of the player and the team he was drafted by. We
figured it might be a pretty long wait until we saw my
name, because the screen would have to show every single team in order with their pick for the first round, then
every team again with their second-round picks, and
again and again, round by round.

But it was exciting to see if there were any names we
knew. I figured there would be, because there was Floyd
Youmans out in California, for example. And I wasn't
even the best-known pitcher in Tampa. The top prospect
had to be Richard Monteleone of Tampa Catholic, who
had gone 14–1 with an ERA of 0.50, while his team won
the state championship. He had gotten more publicity
than I did, plus he was nineteen and I was only seventeen. So I expected him to go a lot higher than me—
maybe even in the first round.

Anyway, the screen started showing the draft, which was being held in New York City, and we settled in. It showed the first pick in the nation was Shawon Dunston, a shortstop, picked by the Cubs. I remembered that. I know I was paying attention to the next few names also, but suddenly they were blotted out of my mind.

On the screen it showed the first round, number-five pick—Dwight Gooden. I saw my name go across, and then New York Mets, and I froze. I couldn't really believe I was actually seeing that. I thought I was dreaming. I asked the guy to please call New York right away and be sure it was correct, that it was me, that there wasn't some other Dwight Gooden someplace, or a mistake on the computer.

He called New York and it was correct. The Mets had picked me fifth in the entire nation. People who worked there at the Tampa *Tribune* all came around and started congratulating me, and I didn't know what to say or do. They asked me how I felt, and I was just shocked. I never kept up with the Mets, didn't even know they had spring training in St. Pete. I was never even talked to by a scout of the Mets, as far as I can remember.

Then I got real excited. I tried to call home, but the line was busy. I kept trying and it stayed busy. I wanted to get home right away and tell my parents. I let my friend drive. We had borrowed my father's car, but I was too excited to drive it home.

When I got home, my father already knew I had been drafted because some radio guy had called. He was as excited as I was, but we couldn't talk much because the phone was ringing all the time. Radio and TV stations were calling—interviews with Channel 13, Channel 8, lots of reporters from papers like the Tampa *Times,* the St. Pete paper, a whole lot of press. A guy called from a

New York paper and I talked to him for a while. I can't even remember which paper it was.

Then my friend Floyd Youmans called from California. He was excited too. He said he'd just been drafted by the Mets. I thought he was just teasing because he'd found out *I'd* been drafted by the Mets. I asked him what round. He said second, they had told him. I asked him if he knew I had gotten drafted by the Mets, too. He asked me what round. I said first. And he didn't believe *me.* We each thought the other was teasing because he hadn't been watching the draft come across the computer so he hadn't seen my name, and I hadn't waited for the second round to see his. When it came out in the papers, then we knew for sure. We were both in the Mets' organization. The Mets had picked me first and him second, and we would be starting out together in the Rookie League.

Things started moving fast. Right away we started getting calls from agents wanting to represent me. My father picked out a few who sounded interesting, and we invited about four over at different times to talk about it. We decided to go with Jim Neader, a lawyer from St. Pete. Jim said that he would make sure that the contract would leave me set up so that once I got out of the game I could be financially secure for life.

Contract negotiations went pretty quickly. I got drafted on June 7, and on June 15 I had to report to Kingsport, Tennessee, to the Appalachian League, for rookie ball. The Mets people had come to my house on June 10. The director of scouting for the Mets, Joe McIlvaine, was there, and the Florida scout, Carlos Pascual.

My salary was $600 a month. For the first year, everybody got $600 a month, whether you started off in a Rookie League or Triple-A. Negotiations were just for the signing bonus. Jim Neader handled that. They started out offering $40,000. That could sound like a lot of money, you know, with me being only seventeen and just coming out of high school. But then I started thinking about being a first-round pick. I knew that Vance Lovelace got drafted in the first round the year before, the twenty-first pick in the first round, and he got $60,000. So since I was the fifth pick, I should be worth a little more than that. We settled on $85,000. And we got it into the contract that if I wanted to go to college sometime, the Mets would take care of the expenses.

I couldn't believe it when I got around to actually signing the contract. I felt as though I was in a dream.

It was a lot of money. It felt great having it, although actually I didn't get the money until later. You get half after you sign and the second half in January, so the taxes won't be so bad. The first check wouldn't come for two weeks. I had already picked out the car I wanted, a silver Camaro Z28. I had enough clothes, from going to high school. I told my parents and sisters they would get some of the money, and some would go to a couple of other relatives. Everybody was excited and happy. It made me feel really good to be able to give out some money, and it helped them. The rest of the money we put away. Jim invested it in some stocks, like oil.

By the time the first check came, I had gone to Kingsport. That week between getting drafted and reporting to Kingsport was over before I knew it.

Going away was not so easy. It didn't really hit me until that day when we were at the airport. The Mets had given me a first-class ticket—the first time I ever flew first class. But that was also the first time I was leaving home for such a long time. The longest I was ever gone before was about two weeks when we went to the Senior League World Series.

I was ready to get on the plane. I looked back. My parents were there, and my sisters and some of my friends, and they were waving. It was a strange feeling. A couple of tears came down my face. I didn't want them to see that, so I just waved and went on in and got on the plane. And when I was in the air I opened up a magazine to read, trying to get my mind off leaving.

Once I got to Kingsport, I saw Floyd Youmans, and that made it easier because we had grown up together and were on the same team in high school. He had left in my junior year so I hadn't seen him for a year. Now we were on the same team in the Rookie League. He was the only guy I knew, but that made it a lot better, starting off together in pro ball.

They had this real big house they rented for a bunch of players, about eight of us. It had six or seven bedrooms, refrigerators, two stoves, an upstairs and a downstairs. It was nice. The landlord stayed in a place in back of our house, on the other side of a little dirt road. He had a garage where he had a phone, and any time we wanted to use the phone we could just go in there and use it. He rented us his truck also. We used that to go to the ballpark, about forty-five minutes away.

It was pretty weird, that time there, being away from home, making our own food. We had a lot of good conversations, getting to know each other, all of us just starting out in pro ball.

Everybody tried to find out what the others had signed for. If a player got, say, $40,000, he might say he got $70,000 and if he'd have held out he might have got more, and so forth. They'd ask me if I had gotten a good contract. I'd say, yeah, but if I'd have held out I probably could've got more. And they'd say, what was the figure? Six-figure or what? And I'd say, between 70 and 100, just leave it at that. That year I got the highest figure there. They usually try to sign the highest pick first, then they'll know how to go about it with the other players. Usually everybody got paid according to how high they got picked, so these guys probably knew I got the most.

I got off to a great start in Kingsport. In my first game I pitched seven innings of shutout ball. It looked to me like pro ball wasn't going to be hard at all. Then in my second game I really got hit hard—seven runs in two innings, including two or three home runs.

I thought: God, what's going on? I thought maybe I had lost all my stuff. But the catcher said my fastball was popping and my curve was breaking well. I figured if my pitches were good, I couldn't lose. But they hit everything I threw.

That night I called my dad in Tampa. I was feeling pretty down. We had a long talk. He reminded me of some things he had told me before, like some days, no matter how well you do, you lose. You put it behind you and come back tomorrow. I wanted to be a perfectionist, but that didn't mean I was going to win every game.

Things turned out to be a little rough in Kingsport, because the team wasn't that great. At one stretch we lost 16 games in a row, and we were in last place, about 16 to 17 games out. But I was throwing the ball well, and had good stuff. They had somebody with a speed gun clocking the velocity of my fastball. The hardest I threw back then was about 92 miles per hour. I throw faster now— my hardest this year was 96—but back then they were happy with my speed and my curveball.

Davey Johnson was a roving instructor in the Mets farm system that year, 1982. One time he asked me about my grips.

I don't have the same grips on the ball as some other pitchers. Most hard throwers, like Nolan Ryan or J. R. Richards, hold the fastball across the seams to get that extra pop. I have two different grips for my fastball. As a right-handed pitcher, if I want the ball to tail away from a right-handed batter, I'll hold the ball across the seams. If I want it to tail in, I'll hold it along the seams. But it also depends on what's working. If I'm holding it across the seams and it's not getting as much movement as I like, I go with the seams. But I have more speed with a grip across the seams—a little extra skip, maybe even a rise. Probably that's because when I'm gripping it across the seams the tips of my fingers can flip up on the threads and sort of whip it. When I'm with the seams, it's more like a sinker.

For my curveball, I have my fingers across the seams— never with the seams. But while I have my fingers together for the fastball, I have them split a little bit apart for the curve. It just works better for some reason. Some people say that's because with the fingers split, some air gets in under them. I never understood that. I just know it has good velocity going down.

Davey seemed to be sort of surprised that I had given so much thought to my grips. But I was always trying to do everything I could to throw the best pitches I could throw.

Besides getting pitching experience, the main thing I was learning in the Rookie League was how to manage being away from your home and family and being on your own. That was a big experience for me. It was the first time traveling with a team, being around players all the time, going to the ballpark all the time. Traveling was tough. We traveled in school buses. The next year, when I went up to Class A and Triple-A, we had better buses, like Greyhounds, and then with the Mets it was airplanes. But in the Rookie League, we had yellow school buses that were cramped, with not much room to stretch out and relax.

I pitched for Kingsport until August 3. My record was only 5–4, but I was doing okay because my ERA was 2.57,

I threw 2 shutouts, and had 66 strikeouts in 66 innings. I made the All-Star team and was named the best pitcher in the Appalachian League.

Early in August they decided to send me up to Little Falls, New York, near Utica, in the New York–Penn League. That was also a Rookie League, but was a little higher up, and Little Falls was in a pennant race with a good chance to win it. So the Mets' organization brought me up there to help.

I wasn't too comfortable in Little Falls. I didn't know one single person. If I had gone to spring training that year, I would have gotten to know some players throughout the organization, because spring training is in the same St. Petersburg complex for all the Mets' teams. But I went directly to Kingsport. I knew Youmans there, and then I got to know all the players pretty well.

But when I moved up to Little Falls, I didn't know anybody on the team, anybody in town. It was like going off to Japan or something. I didn't know anything. So it was pretty tough in that way.

Also, there were only two blacks on the team—me and Johnny Wilson, Mookie Wilson's younger brother. When I went there I thought maybe it was going to be pretty tough just for that reason. But everybody on the team treated me fine: racially there was no difference.

But in the town, which is small, there were no blacks. In Kingsport, I'd say we had about eight blacks on the team, and the town had quite a few blacks. But I did not see one black person in Little Falls, outside our team. That was the first time I'd been in that situation.

I felt uncomfortable away from the ballpark. At nighttime, a couple of players asked me if I wanted to go out with them and have a couple of drinks, and I said sure. But where we went, a lot of people stared. Nobody said anything, but they looked at me. I was staying at a hotel, and when I walked through the hotel, some people used to call me names. I guess they didn't know I played ball.

I tried not to pay any attention. When I was playing, I couldn't really concentrate on what I had to do because of the little fear that was in me. In the town, when I walked around, it was there. Partly, I guess, because I was only seventeen, and it was my first time away from home.

Every day I used to call my friends back home. I would talk to them for a while until it was time to go to the ballpark. I told my parents about how I felt, and my father asked me if any players were giving me trouble. I said no, the players were great to me. But outside the ballpark was different. He told me to talk to the manager, Sam Perlozzo. I wanted to go to him, but being so quiet, I didn't know how to just come off and talk to him at that time. So I didn't say anything at all.

I was there two weeks, two long weeks. When we went on the road, I was really happy to travel. I didn't help the team much. I made 2 starts, gave up 6 runs in 13 innings, and had a record of 0–1.

After about the fifth inning of the second game, my arm started bothering me, getting tired, not feeling quite right. I told them I didn't want to take a chance with it. When Steve Schryver, the minor league director, came into town, I told him my arm was tired.

He sent me to New York to see Dr. Parkes, the Mets' team doctor. He told me it was probably tendinitis, just from having thrown so many innings that year, including high school and pro. So they let me go home.

But before I left New York I saw a couple of games at Shea Stadium. I sat in a booth high up over the field. I had never been in a major league ballpark before, and this was really beautiful. It made me want to work all the harder to get to the big leagues.

Thinking back, I don't really blame Little Falls for

anything. I was very young, and they just hadn't seen many blacks. Anyway, I never ran into that problem again.

In the fall, I pitched in the Instructional League for a while, working on a few things. George Bamberger, who was then the Mets' manager, came down, and so did John Cumberland, who was pitching coach at Lynchburg in the Class A Carolina League.

Then in March of 1983, spring training started, and they told me I had moved up to Columbia, South Carolina, in the Class A South Atlantic League. That was exciting, knowing that I had moved up a step, and I was thrilled to be on the Columbia roster. They said they had a complex right next to a college campus that was real nice, so I was looking forward to that. I worked out with Columbia in the spring training complex in St. Pete.

But the last week of spring training, I got moved up again. They assigned me to Lynchburg, which was higher in Class A ball. So I was even happier to be going there.

My salary went up to $800 a month. After taxes and everything it was about $245 every two weeks. That was okay, I could get by on that.

The players in Class A were older. In the Rookie Leagues the oldest were probably twenty-one or twenty-two. At Lynchburg, the oldest were maybe twenty-four. And they were tougher hitters.

I started out the season with Lynchburg pitching sort of mediocrely—3–2 in my first eight starts. Then we came up to Shea Stadium to play the Salem Redbirds, the Texas Rangers' Class A team, in a kind of exhibition game for the fans before the Mets played the Padres. It was a regular season game for us, but playing in Shea, my first time playing on a major league field, made it specially exciting. I was pretty pumped up. It was so exciting just being there that it was kind of hard to concentrate on the game.

Another reason I was pumped up was that the two teams didn't like each other too much. Earlier in the season, in a game I wasn't pitching, their pitcher hit one of our batters, and then our pitcher hit one of their batters, and we had a big brawl. I got involved with everybody else, just trying to stop it, and another guy and I ended up throwing a couple of punches at each other. I didn't get thrown out of the game, though.

And then in a later game, when I was pitching, I tried to brush back one of their batters with a fastball, just to intimidate him, trying to warn them not to throw at our hitters, but I hit the guy. The batter didn't do anything, but the umpire came out and talked to me, warning me. So our team and their team never got along too well.

In this game at Shea, as I say, I was pumped up and throwing out great pitches. I had a one-hitter and 14 strikeouts going into the ninth, and we were winning, 1–0. Then they got a dinky scratch hit in the infield, then a bunt hit, and then a hit up the middle to score a run and tie the game.

I was still throwing well. I struck out the next guy. But the guy after that came up and hit a home run. When he went around the bases, he was pointing at me, trying to show me up. And his team was yelling and pointing, all trying to show me up.

What with what had happened before in the season, and now losing my shutout, and probably the game, since we were behind 4–1, and this guy trying to show me up, I got a little hot.

Before I threw the next pitch, I figured something was probably going to happen, because I was going to throw it right at the batter's ribs. Instead, I ended up hitting him in the neck. The guy fell, the trainer came out. The guy got up and just looked at the mound. I thought maybe he was going to charge me. I took off my glove and just stared at him. And I stared into their dugout, just waiting. But nothing happened, and the umpire didn't say anything.

Then our manager, Sam Perlozzo, came and took me out. So I lost that game. But then I won 15 games in a row. I didn't lose for about three months, until Salem beat me again in late August.

Along the way, I came the closest I had ever come in the minors to a no-hitter. We were playing Peninsula, the Phillies' farm team, and we were home in Lynchburg, so I had the crowd behind me. I had only given up two walks, and had two outs in the ninth. I had struck out the first two guys in the ninth, giving me 15 for the game, and after I struck out those guys, I said, I know I can get it now.

Al LeBoeuf came up, one of the toughest hitters in the league. After I had come that far, and a lot of our players had made great plays behind me the whole game, I was sure it would go my way, and if he hit the ball, it would be at somebody.

I got two strikes on LeBoeuf. Two strikes, two outs. I wanted to get him with a fastball. I reared back and let it go with all I had. He hit a ball with eyes. It was a chopper right over my head, right up the middle, and the short-stop couldn't quite get to it.

That hit was so depressing that I was kind of hoping the manager would come and take me out right then. But he didn't. And the next batter almost hit a home run off me. Our center fielder made a great catch at the fence, to end it and save the shutout and the win.

Lynchburg had won the first-half title, and were on the verge of winning the second half also. Hagerstown came in, the Orioles' farm club. We needed to win one out of three from them. I beat them the first game, so that gave us the second half.

The next day I was sent up to Tidewater for the Triple-A play-offs and world series. The Mets had called up Ron Darling, so I filled his spot at Tidewater.

It was very exciting to go up there to Triple-A for the championship series, but it was a little tough also, because I learned right away that the batters were more selective and didn't swing at as many pitches out of the strike zone as they had at Lynchburg.

My first game was against Columbus, the Yankees' team. I threw the ball well for four innings. Steve Balboni was their big home run threat, and the player with the biggest reputation that I had ever faced. I knew that I had to concentrate a little bit more on him. He flied out once and I struck him out once.

But in the fifth inning I gave up a walk, then two home runs—one to Butch Hobson, who had been up with the Angels, and one to Brian Dayett, who was about to go up to the Yankees. So I pitched five innings and gave up three earned runs, and we lost my first Triple-A championship game, 5–3.

After that, I faced Richmond, the Braves' team, pitched a complete game, and beat them 6–1—they got one unearned run. That clinched the International League title, and we advanced to the Triple-A World Series at Louisville.

The world series was three teams in a kind of round-robin—us, Denver of the American Association, which is the White Sox's team, and Portland of the Pacific Coast League, which is the Phillies' team. I pitched another complete game against Portland and beat them 4–2. We won the world series and were champs of the minor leagues.

So I finished up 1983 with a record of 19–4 at Lynchburg and the league record of 300 strikeouts, and was 2–1 in the Triple-A championship series. I figured that was a good year for me.

After that, there was no doubt in my mind I could pitch major league ball, as long as I stayed healthy and worked at it. My rookie year I had kind of wondered how long it would take, but in that second year things started coming around for me.

Still, before spring training of 1984, before anybody talked to me about contracts or anything, I figured I would probably pitch at Tidewater that year. I would go there for at least a couple of starts, or to the All-Star break, and then if I was throwing the ball well, maybe then I'd get a shot at the big leagues.

CHAPTER 3

February–May, 1984

By spring training of 1984, in February, I was really ready to work hard and see where I would end up. They brought me in to pitch with the big league club, as a nonroster player. I thought they were just bringing me there for experience, and maybe because they had lost Tom Seaver to the White Sox, and they were looking over a few people as a possible replacement.

The pitchers came in a week early, so I got to know them. The Mets had a lot of young pitchers, like Darling and Terrell and Tim Leary, along with veterans like Craig Swan and Ed Lynch and Mike Torrez, and good relievers like Jesse Orosco and Doug Sisk. There were also some guys with great potential, like Sid Fernandez, whom the Mets got from the Dodgers' organization in the off-season, and Calvin Schiraldi, who was with Jackson in Double A.

But when the other players came in, I didn't know them well. They were pretty much strangers. Davey Johnson, who had managed at Tidewater, was the new Mets manager.

The first major leaguer I ever pitched to was in an intrasquad game. It was Wally Backman, a Mets infielder

I had played with in the Tidewater championships before he was called up. I was kind of nervous, because a lot of coaches and brass were watching around the fence. Even Frank Cashen, the Mets' general manager, was there. So even though this was just an intrasquad game, I was trying to do great.

I walked Backman. Then I struck out shortstop Ron Gardenhire and outfielder Danny Heep on curveballs and third baseman Hubie Brooks with fastballs.

I felt great, mainly because nobody had scored off me. In the second inning, I gave up a walk, a hit, and a run. In the third I shut them out.

Before I pitched, nobody said too much to me. But after that, players opened up and teased me and were pretty friendly.

I pitched three innings of a "B" game against the Cardinals, a mixture of reserves and regulars, and gave up three hits. Then my first "A" game start, against a regular major league team, came against the Toronto Blue Jays.

It was in Dunedin, which is pretty close to Tampa, in a stadium where I had pitched in high school tournaments. My parents came, and a lot of friends. Guys from my high school came, guys who were sophomores when I was a senior at Hillsborough, guys who I used to play with on the same field. Just two years after I had played with them, and we were all dreaming of being major leaguers, they were sitting in the stands paying to watch *me* play. It gave me a strange feeling, something to think about.

I was nervous going into the game, facing big league hitters I didn't know, who weren't on my team, players I had only watched on TV. I told myself: Just throw strikes, you got to start somewhere, and this is a good time to start and get prepared for the season.

I had jitters, but I was throwing strikes. The first batter

I faced was Willie Upshaw, and I got him on a ground ball. Then with Ernie Witt, I got the count to 2–2. I tried to give him a fastball low, but I got it up, and he hit a double over Mookie Wilson's head in center field.

Then Cliff Johnson was up. I knew he was a big power hitter. I started with a fastball, and he swung late. Then he took a curve for a ball. I tried to go up and in with a fastball, but it went down the middle, and Johnson hit it over the center field fence for a home run.

After he hit that, I was a little intimidated and started to overthrow. But I retired the next eight in a row, and the last was Witt. This time I got him to swing at a 3–2 curveball for a strikeout.

The nail on my index finger had split a couple of days earlier, and it had started bleeding. Also, my lower back was stiffening up. Davey took me out. I figured Davey hadn't been expecting too much in my first game, just wanted to see what my reactions would be in facing big league players. I knew somebody was going to hit me pretty hard in my first game. I was trying to do a little bit too much, I guess, and impress the brass because I wanted to make the team. I wanted to be perfect, but I figured I would make some mistake pitches, which I did. But I figured I had done a pretty good job over all.

Next time out I pitched four innings against the Blue Jays, gave up two hits and no walks, and struck out three.

About a week before spring training ended, I started against the Yankees in Fort Lauderdale. That was a turning point. George Steinbrenner, who owns the Yankees, was at the game. He also lives in Tampa and everybody in Tampa knows about him. I never thought about joining the Yankees, but during the off-season, Billy Reed, my high school coach, who knows him pretty well, told me that Steinbrenner had said he was going to do everything he could to get me.

This was a very big game for me, starting in front of the biggest crowd of spring training—maybe 30,000—against the Yankees. The game was being televised back to New York. Ron Guidry was going for the Yankees, and he was the biggest name pitcher I had worked against to that point. Just the idea of the two of us starting out against each other was a thrill. And watching him pitch, I was very impressed. Smart pitcher. I saw he wasn't afraid to throw off-speed pitches in tough situations. Even though he had a good fastball, he didn't always go right at the hitters. Lots of times he went with locations and curveballs.

I pitched five innings and had command of my pitches and threw well. I gave up three hits and one run. Graig Nettles hit a home run, and that was off a great pitch—a change-up down and in. He golfed it out of the park. I found out later that he's a good off-speed hitter and he likes the ball down there, but I didn't know it then.

Craig Swan finished up. We won it in the ninth, 4–1.

Right then I thought maybe I made the team, because I gave up only one run to the Yankees, and by then the Mets had already made a lot of cuts in the roster and I was one of the last extra pitchers they still had there.

The press was starting to write a lot about how I might make the team, or I should make the team. They were comparing me to Nolan Ryan and Bob Gibson and stars like that, how I was like them in their early years. One reporter was trying to get me to say I was the best pitcher in the organization, that I should make the team with no problem. He couldn't get it out of me, because I wouldn't say stuff like that. So he wrote that the Mets' front office had ordered me to keep my mouth shut, which wasn't true. All they had ever told me was to just be myself.

I knew Davey Johnson was planning to go with a young

staff. We had ten pitchers and he was saying he would be taking nine pitchers up. The press was speculating that either Tim Leary or I would go to Tidewater. But nobody was telling me anything, so I had to try and block it out of my mind as much as I could, because I didn't want to be too disappointed if I didn't make it.

There was also a lot of speculation on who would be the catcher for the Mets. Who catches you is very important. Of course you want a catcher who can field and hit and throw. But you also want a guy back there who can communicate with you, understand what pitches you like to throw in certain situations, and can steady you and keep your confidence up and keep you on the right track. John Stearns had been having trouble with an elbow injury for a long time, and was put on the Disabled List. John Gibbons, who was with Jackson in Double-A ball, had been catching a lot of games, and toward the end of spring training it looked like he might make the Mets.

But a few days before spring training was over, Gibbons was hurt in a collision at home plate; he broke his cheekbone. So until he could heal, the catcher with the Mets would probably be either Mike Fitzgerald, who had caught me at Tidewater and then went up with the Mets at the end of the season last year, or Junior Ortiz, whom the Mets got from Pittsburgh.

On the last day of spring training, the last game, I pitched one inning against the Tigers. I faced three hitters, got one on a fly ball, and struck out two.

Then, in the dugout, Davey told me I had made the team. He was taking all ten pitchers up north with the Mets, and I was the fourth starter.

So now, here we were, leading the National League East, and I had won my first start at Houston and was ready to go in my second, against the Chicago Cubs.

In a way, it was a lot easier making the team than I thought it would be, because in the beginning just being around big league players was intimidating—some of them were twice my age. So I hadn't thought it would be this quick. But then I had won my first start, and now the team was on a roll.

From what I had heard from players about the year before, there was a different attitude in the Mets now. Players told me they had a good team in 1983, but some of them were just showing up at the ballpark, not caring too much whether they won or lost, just glad to get the games over and get their checks and go home. Too many just wanted their money.

I was making $40,000 for the year. That doesn't sound like a lot as far as big league money is concerned, but your first year in the big leagues you're going to start out at the $40,000 minimum, and that was a lot better than I was getting in the minor leagues. And if you do well, the big numbers are going to come.

But anyway, that wasn't as important to me as winning ball games, because I really hate to lose. So I was glad to see a different attitude with the Mets when I came up. Nobody wanted to be on a losing team, and now we were winning.

We were 6–1 when we went into Wrigley Field, where I would pitch the opening game of the series against the Cubs. The Cubs were 3–4. I knew they had been struggling just like the Mets the last couple years, so going into the game I was a little more relaxed than at Houston. But I was still nervous. I'd have been more nervous if I had known what was going to happen.

It was a big crowd for the Cubs' first game at home, and the crowd was really behind them. They hit me right away in the first inning. I started out walking Bob Dernier. Then Ryne Sandberg got a single. Gary Matthews got a double, and Sandberg scored. Davey was pretty patient, and he let me stay in there. I got them out, and except for that one run, held them scoreless until the fourth. Steve Trout was shutting us out also.

I didn't have much of a fastball that day; it was staying up a lot. Chicago has a low pitchers' mound. They don't have anybody who throws a real hard fastball, but they have a lot of sinkerball pitchers. So they have the flat mound and the high grass in the infield, because they get a lot of ground balls and that way the balls won't go through the infield too quickly. The low mound isn't good for me.

I was walking a lot of people. They were stealing bases, too. I have a high leg kick that gives runners a jump, and I wasn't holding them on base successfully. My catcher was John Gibbons, who had joined the club after his injury healed. He told me to take my time and settle down, and concentrate more on keeping the ball down.

In the fourth, they loaded the bases with no outs. They were hitting me and getting on base, so I figured I had to change something. Instead of going with my best pitches, I tried to trick the hitters. So I was giving them *their* pitch to hit instead of making them hit *my* pitch, and that was getting me in a lot of trouble.

Larry Bowa hit a single over short, driving in two runs. Then Trout bunted down the third base line. I didn't field it the way you're supposed to. When they square around to bunt, you're supposed to charge. But I just watched the pitch go instead of charging over to field it. I usually fielded well, but it was as though I wasn't myself, as though I was in somebody else's control. By the time I picked up the bunt, there was nothing I could do with it, and the bases were loaded again.

Dernier grounded to second on a fielder's choice,

scoring another run. Sandberg hit a two-run double. The score was 6–0.

Mel Stottlemyre, the pitching coach, came out to the mound. He told me that I'd had enough, and Davey was going to make a move. He was just coming out first to give Ed Lynch a little more time to get ready in the bullpen. Stottlemyre went back to the dugout, and Davey came out. When he got to the mound, he said he was going with Lynch now, and I should just hang with it and get them next time.

I waited for Lynch to get about halfway in from the bullpen, then I took off and trotted to the dugout. I usually walk off, but this was my first time being knocked out of a game in the big leagues, and I just wanted to hurry up and get off the field.

The Cubs were jumping up and down and yelling and giving high fives, the crowd was cheering and screaming, and I felt awful. Davey followed me off the field, and he patted me on the rear and said, "Bob Gibson got his butt kicked sometimes too. You'll be okay, don't worry about it."

We ended up losing, 11–2, my first loss.

That was the hardest I had gotten hit and the earliest I had gotten taken out since my first year in rookie ball. Getting blown away like that, suddenly I wondered if I was really ready for the big leagues after all, or if I should go down to Triple-A. Maybe I needed more time in the minors. I thought about how well I had pitched in Houston, and figured maybe I had been pitching over my head.

Stottlemyre talked to me after the game. He said that as long as you're playing, things like that can happen— even two or three times in a row—and that I shouldn't let any team or hitter intimidate me. He said not to let one bad outing turn my season around, and that he knew I could pitch in the big leagues, and I should believe in myself.

I thought a lot about it. I called my father, who had seen the game on cable TV. He said I should just put it behind me and learn from my mistakes and get ready to pitch next time.

So that night I watched TV and listened to music and tried to think about other things. I told myself: If you lose, or everything you throw is hit, you don't want to let that mess everything up. It's over, there's nothing you can do about it.

By the next day I had just about put it out of my mind. But then there was an article in the paper where they had me quoted as saying that the Cubs were "hot dogs." That was the most embarrassing thing that came out about me in a newspaper all year. I did tell a reporter that when the Cubs beat me they were jumping up and down and cheering and acting like it was the World Series, and I didn't like it. He asked me if I thought the Cubs were hotdogging it, and I said, "I don't know, maybe they're trying to pump up the crowd for the first home game." Then I read in the paper that Gooden called the Cubs hot dogs, which I didn't. I wouldn't call them any names.

It really bothered me, to read that. I was in batting practice before the next day's game, and Larry Bowa, the Cubs' shortstop, came up and asked me if I had said the Cubs were hot dogs. I said no, I was misquoted. He said he figured that's what happened, because he figured I was a better guy than that. He believed me, he said, because he knew how reporters could be at times.

So everything was cleared up about that, and it was okay. Other than that, the press was treating me great.

The Cubs beat us again, 5–2, so the team was a little down at the end of our long road trip. But we were heading home now to Shea Stadium, and we were still in

first place, so our spirits were pretty good when we got to
New York.

Over at Shea, people had set up our lockers and everything, and the team had the players' cars brought up
from Florida. I had arranged for an apartment in Port
Washington, on Long Island, but it wasn't ready yet, so I
stayed at the Marriott Hotel across the highway from
LaGuardia Airport, near the stadium.

Hubie Brooks showed me around the city a little.
Some people had advised me to avoid places like Harlem
and certain parts of the Bronx and Queens. No matter
where you go, whether it's Miami or New York or wherever, there's going to be some bad places. But the way
some people talked about it, some of these places in New
York were so bad that if you went in there you wouldn't
come out. Just by going around, I found out that it's not
as bad as those people said it was. I didn't go into the city
much anyway. Mainly those first days I just stayed at the
hotel or the stadium.

But Hubie did take me out one time to a disco, Studio
54. I had never heard of Studio 54 and had never been in
a club like that. It was strange. Hubie knew a lot of
people, and he introduced me around. People didn't
know who I was then, when he introduced me. It wasn't
like now. People didn't start knowing me until late June
or July. I don't dance at all, but I liked going and listening to the music, because I love music. And it was nice
just being away from the hotel.

When I was at Shea for the first time as a Met, not too
many people knew me. Lots of people thought I was
Darryl Strawberry. We're both pretty tall and lean. When
we were having batting practice for the home opener
against the Montreal Expos, a guy called to me, "Hey,
Strawberry!" He wanted my autograph. I said, "I'm not
Strawberry, I'm Gooden." He said, "Come on, Straw-

berry, you just don't want to sign. You're not Gooden." I
said, "Well, I'm not Strawberry." And I walked away,
because I didn't want to sign my real name, which might
make him angry or something, and I didn't want to sign
Strawberry's name. Later on in the season, people
started calling Strawberry "Gooden," and he didn't sign
either.

The year before, when I was with Lynchburg and after
we came to Shea to play that one game, I was always
dreaming about playing there and coming to the stadium
every day. Now I was actually there, in that big stadium,
and there was a big crowd. I enjoyed just looking at the
crowd and watching the fans.

They had more than 46,000 fans there for opening
day, and we got blown out, 10–0. The fans started booing. I guess they figured it was the same old Mets. When
they got on us, I thought it was going to be a long season,
especially after the start I had against the Cubs. I was
imagining what they were going to do to me when I
pitched a couple days later.

The night after that first game we had a banquet for
the public to come and welcome the Mets home. Every
season they do that. It helped, after the loss, to have a
banquet. Nelson Doubleday, the owner of the Mets,
spoke, and so did Frank Cashen and Davey Johnson and
some of the players, like Strawberry. Some of the guys
were telling me that the first-year players had to get up
and speak also, although I wasn't in any condition to get
up and speak in front of so many people. But I figured I
had to speak because so much had been written about me
and they probably wanted to know what I had to say.

I was sitting there sweating bullets, trying to think of
something to say, but I couldn't think of one single line.
It turned out they were just teasing me, and I didn't have
to speak, so I got lucky on that one.

The next day we beat the Expos 5–4 when Wally Backman drove in two runs with a two-out double in the ninth.

Then it was time for my first turn at home. We were playing the Expos again. It was a weird feeling walking out to the mound that first time as a Met. Even though I had pitched there the year before with Lynchburg, it was different being in a Mets uniform, and knowing the crowd was there to see me pitch. It was my first time in the major leagues pitching for *my* crowd at home. I wanted to show the fans in Shea that I belonged in the big leagues, especially after what had happened to me in Chicago.

The first guy I faced was Pete Rose, the legend I had always dreamed of playing against. Just looking at him in the batter's box, I was nervous because of who he was. I was so honored facing him that I forgot what I was out there to do, which was get him out.

Keith Hernandez always tried to help me with what to throw the hitters, because he knew them better than I did. He had told me that Rose's hands were not so fast any more and he couldn't really catch up to a good fastball, so I should pitch him hard and in.

Rose was all crouched down and ready. I figured he would hit the ball somewhere, and I hoped it would be at somebody. I threw him a fastball and he swung and fouled it off—which made me jump, because I was so nervous. Next pitch he grounded out to short. When he was thrown out at first and ran back across the infield, I just watched him all the way. I was amazed that I had gotten him out.

I shut them out the first two innings, and we came up with four runs, so I had a little cushion.

In the third, with one out, I got two strikes on Rose and then he singled up the middle. I was annoyed that I had grooved one down the middle to him. I walked Bryan Little on four pitches.

Now I was looking at Tim Raines and then Andre Dawson, two dangerous hitters, with two men on base and only one out. I stepped off the mound to get myself together.

Raines is a good contact hitter, doesn't strike out much, so you've got to be aggressive with him. I started him off with a fastball down the middle and he took it for a strike. I guess he thought with two men on base I was going to be intimidated. He took a fastball away for a ball. I threw the curve; he swung and missed. He took another fastball outside. The count was 2–2.

Gibbons put down the sign for fastball. I didn't want to throw it. I wanted to throw the curve. But I went ahead and threw the fastball anyway. Raines swung and didn't come close.

The crowd cheered and got me pumped up to go even harder.

Now up came Dawson, one of the best players in the game and one of the best fastball hitters. I figured he might be swinging for a home run in that situation. I threw a couple of fastballs and he fouled them off.

Then I called Gibbons to the mound. I told him I was going to waste one more fastball, then throw a curve in the dirt, to see if he'd go for it. So I told him to get ready to block it, and I'd cover home plate in case it got by.

I threw the fastball up and inside, and he took it. Then I threw the curveball. It was in the dirt, but sooner than I meant—out in front of home plate. But Dawson swung way out ahead of it, Gibbons came up with the ball, and we were out of the inning.

We got another run to lead 5–0, and when I went out for the fourth inning I was still pumped up. I struck out Gary Carter on fastballs—although I threw him one change-up that I shouldn't have thrown, and he pulled it long but foul. Then I struck out Tim Wallach on fastballs. And then I struck out Terry Francona, then the league's leading hitter, with a good curve.

I had struck out five Expos in a row, the heart of their batting order, and I couldn't believe I had done it. That gave me a lot of confidence.

But in the fifth I got in trouble again. A couple of hits and a walk, and the bases were loaded with two outs. Dawson hit a ground ball to Gardenhire at short—he had made a great play just before to save me, but this time the ball went right under his glove for an error, and a run scored. Carter singled to left, and two more runs scored. With Wallach, I had already struck him out a couple of times, and I got two strikes on him again. Then I went up and in with a fastball, and he kind of turned and took it on the arm. That was the first time I had hit a batter in the major leagues. It didn't seem like he really tried to avoid it. I figured maybe he just took it for the team. The bases were loaded again. I walked Francona to force in a run.

Finally I got out of the inning with four unearned runs, and we still had the lead, 5–4. Davey took me out then because I had thrown 118 pitches, which was all he wanted me to throw. I had heard about how the New York fans love you one day and hate you the next, and I figured maybe I'd get a lot of boos. But when I came off, a few people clapped and that was about it. I just went straight in to take a shower.

The Expos got two runs in the seventh to take the lead, but Hubie Brooks won it for us with a two-run homer in the eighth. So I got a no-decision, Jesse Orosco got the win. That kept us in first place by half a game over the Phillies.

In a way I felt bad because I didn't get the win, but then again the runs in the fifth inning were unearned, and they didn't start getting hits until after the error. Gardenhire didn't say anything about the error, and I didn't think he should have, either. Nobody tries to make an error, they're professional and that kind of thing's going to happen. No matter what an error costs, I don't expect anybody to come and apologize to me. But later on in the season we used to tease about it now and then.

After that game was the first time I was ever on "Kiner's Korner," the post-game TV show. At the time, all I knew about Kiner was that he broadcast the Mets games. I didn't know anything about him as a baseball player or home run hitter until later in the season when we went to Pittsburgh and they showed old highlights on the big Diamond Vision screen. They showed Ralph Kiner hitting. I was surprised.

That first time on his show, he asked me how it felt making the jump from Class A ball to the big leagues and pitching to hitters I've idolized. I told him it was sure a lot different to be in the big leagues, and I never thought I'd get there so quickly. And I said a lot of times you've got to blank out of your mind who you're pitching against, in the sense of not letting anybody intimidate you. He asked me how it was living in New York, coming from Tampa. I said that Tampa's not real small, but it's real small compared to New York.

I was on that show about six or seven times during the season, always about 15 minutes after a game at Shea, but never after I pitched a loss. When you went on, they gave you a watch, a hundred-dollar bill, and a box of cigars. I used to give the cigars to Frank Howard, our first base coach, because he smoked cigars.

Then we went on the road again, to Philadelphia and Montreal. I felt that I was getting to know my teammates a little better. Some of the veteran players liked to tease me a little in the beginning, saying things like, "How you doing, youngster? You homesick yet?" But mainly they treated me just like everybody else, on and off the field, just like I was their age, and I felt comfortable.

Sometimes there was a little horseplay that I wasn't much a part of early in the season, and it cost us in Philadelphia. In the locker room, some guys were playing Hackey-Sack, where you kick a little beanbag around, and Ron Gardenhire got hit in the eye and hurt, so he couldn't play in the game. I figured Davey Johnson might be pretty hot about that, and he did call a team meeting and said he didn't want any more Hackey-Sacking in the locker room. I wasn't involved in that. Orosco and Fitzgerald had been trying to teach me how to play, but it was too tough.

The Phillies took us two out of three, dropping us to second place, the Expos beat us one game, and then I had my fourth start.

I had a no-hitter going against the Expos for the first five innings. The only base runner had gotten there on a walk, and I picked him off first—the first time I'd picked anybody off base since Little League. I was striking people out. Junior Ortiz was catching that day—Gibbons never did get his bat going—and he knew a lot of the hitters from playing against them last year when he was with the Pirates, so he was helping me mix up pitches well. David Palmer had shut us out so far also.

But Terry Francona led off the sixth with a single, a chopper over my head up the middle, to bust up the no-hitter. Then I balked him to second—the third base umpire ruled I hadn't come to a stop in my stretch before going to the plate. With my problems holding runners on base, I had been thinking too much about Francona trying to steal and not enough about making my pitch.

I struck out Angel Salazar and Palmer. Then Pete Rose hit a ground ball to Backman at second. The field was kind of wet from rain the night before, and either the footing was a little bad or the ball was slick, because Wally threw the ball into the dugout, and Francona scored.

I pitched 7 innings, gave up 2 hits and that unearned run, and struck out 10, which was my most strikeouts so far in the majors. But I left with us behind, 1–0. Doug Sisk relieved me, and then Orosco came in. Rusty Staub tied it up for us with a pinch-hit double in the eighth, and George Foster drove in the winning run in the eleventh. Orosco got his second win, and I got another no-decision.

Back home, we took two out of three from the Phillies and moved into a first-place tie with the Cubs. We had the Cubs next. I would pitch the opener against them, and I really wanted to get even. Mostly what I had against the Cubs was getting my first loss against them in Chicago, when they got six runs in three innings, and the way they had stolen bases on me and had given high fives and fired up the crowd and rubbed it in. So I was really pumped up for this game, not only for those reasons, but because we were playing for first place. They were going to be ready to swing the bat, and I wasn't going to let them pound me like last time.

The crowds were smaller this time at home—only about 14,000 for this game. But that actually helped my confidence. If I did anything wrong, there weren't too many people to boo me. As the season went on, and the whole thing with my strikeouts began building up, I got to where I needed lots of fans to cheer me on. But right now, small was fine. I just wanted to get the ball and get at the Cubs.

I heard the noise from the crowd right away in the first inning with the first hitter, when I got two strikes on Dernier. Fans started standing up and yelling for a strikeout. That was the first time that had happened. I guess they had read about the game in Montreal where I had 10 strikeouts, and maybe they were hoping I would replace Tom Seaver in that category. I had to remind myself not to overthrow, just make good pitches and let the strikeouts come.

But by being so anxious to pay them back for what they did to me in Chicago, I started right off overthrowing the fastball to Dernier, and my pitches were up. I walked him, he stole second, and Fitzgerald's throw went into center field, so Dernier went to third.

I was a little shook up about that. I thought: Uh-oh, here comes the same thing that happened last time. But then I told myself I'm just going to throw strikes. I figured with a man on third and no outs, Dernier's going to get in anyway. But I'm going to go pretty hard at the next hitter, Sandberg.

Sandberg fouled off two fastballs. He's a right-handed hitter, and I remembered the last time I faced him with a man in scoring position. He had been late on my fastball and tried to go to the opposite field, but he had pulled my curveball for a double. I figured right here is a curveball situation, but I'm going to go with a fastball. So I went with a fastball inside on him and tied him up. There was nothing he could do except look. He took it for strike three.

Then Matthews. In Chicago, Matthews had hit my off-speed pitches pretty well—hit a curve and a change-up for hits—and was late on my fastball. So now I would stay with my fastball until he showed me he could hit that. He fouled a couple off, then I went upstairs with a fastball, and he looked at it for strike three also. A couple of times later in the game I showed him the off-speed ball in the dirt, just to see if he'd go for it, but I never threw it anywhere he could handle it. I struck him out twice that game with upstairs fastballs.

Now with two outs and Dernier still on third, I got Bill Buckner on a groundout to get out of the inning.

I struck out six in the first three innings. Dick Ruthven was pitching pretty well against us too, and it was a pitcher's game until the sixth. They got one run on a couple of hits, and we got seven.

I came out after 7 innings with 4 hits and 10 strikeouts. Sisk finished up. We won 8–1, and I had my second win.

It was also the second straight time I had struck out ten hitters, but I didn't know how many I had until after the game, when reporters brought it up. They told me it was the first time a Met pitcher had struck out ten twice in a row since Seaver in 1975. It was great to know that I had done that. To strike out ten batters two games in a row, that's something you can always look back on.

Also, the reporters told me I was third in strikeouts in the league now behind Ryan and Fernando Valenzuela. I had 36, Valenzuela had 38, and Ryan 39. I was really excited about being third behind two of the top strikeout pitchers in the league. That was just like being in first place to me.

And we were in first place also. That win put us a game up on Chicago.

CHAPTER 4

May 6–June 15

For three or four days before the Sunday game when I would be going up against Nolan Ryan for the first time, the press had been coming at me asking how I felt about it. They were talking about how the fans would be coming out to see strikeouts. They were trying to build it up to a real big confrontation and making it sound like it was just me against Ryan, like a tennis match or something. I said it would be an honor for me to pitch against Ryan, somebody I have always looked up to and was compared to when I was coming up through Little League and high school. But I was trying to get across to them that I couldn't just have my mind on Ryan, because it would be me against the whole Astros team, and Ryan couldn't hurt me with the bat. I just hoped my hitters could get more runs off him than his hitters got off me.

I didn't really like the way the game was being built up, but then again I figured because it was me against Ryan it would probably be a low-scoring game, so it did make a difference that it was Ryan pitching. I had to keep his team from scoring many runs, because we weren't going to get many. I hoped we could score two or three runs, so if I could hold them to one or two we could win.

We had split the first two games of the series. Darling shut them out, 2–0, on two hits in one, and then they scored four runs off Orosco in the eighth to win 10–6 in the other, But we were still in first place by a game over the Cubs, two games over the Phillies, and three over the Expos.

I wanted to take it as just another game and not think about Ryan. The main thing was to stay within myself and throw strikes. I didn't want to try to strike everybody out. I just wanted to throw good pitches and get hitters out any way I could. (It's a whole lot easier on my arm if they hit the first or second pitch and make an out than for me to have to go through more pitches to strike them out.)

But I think now I put a little pressure on myself that I shouldn't have. I guess all that hype did have an effect on me. I worried about who I was pitching against, and I got to overthrowing and trying too hard and not pitching my game. That's why I came out of the game pretty early.

There were 40,000 fans out there to watch, and I pitched two pretty good innings. I struck out two batters in the first. The fans really got into it. We got a couple of hits and a run in our half. In the second I struck out another batter.

For the first time I noticed that not only did the fans start yelling for a strikeout as soon as I got a couple of strikes on the batter, now some of them in the outfield were hanging out big red "K" signs over the railing with every strikeout I got. I didn't want to get caught up in what they had out there, so I tried not to look around at it.

In the bottom of the second, with us leading 1–0, I had my first chance to bat against Ryan. We had a man on first and one out, and I was sent up there to sacrifice bunt and move our runner to second.

Mookie Wilson had told me earlier in the season that someday when I batted against Ryan and his fastball, I'd know how hitters felt when they were facing me. Now I went up there to face the toughest pitcher I had ever seen. I was struggling with bunting early in the season. Later on I got it straightened out and usually got the job done. This time I was nervous.

Ryan went into the stretch and I squared around to bunt. Fastball, and I fouled it back. But that pitch had been coming pretty well, and I was more nervous. Second fastball; I stuck out the bat and didn't come close. With two strikes, third base coach Bobby Valentine gave me the signal to hit away.

Ryan came with his third fastball, hard and high. It was right there in a hurry; I swung and was happy just to connect with it. It was a grounder to short, a double-play ball. I ran it out hard, trying to beat the double play, but they got it.

Coming back to the dugout, I said to Mookie and the others, "Now I know what it probably feels like hitting against myself." They laughed, and somebody said that Ryan wasn't throwing his best to me because I'm only a pitcher. I said, "If that wasn't his best, then he should be unhittable. At least he didn't strike me out."

I was out of breath from running so hard. But instead of taking some time and getting a towel to dry off, I got my glove and went straight to the mound to pitch. That was inexperience, and it was a mistake I wouldn't make again in the season. I was still breathing hard when I started to pitch.

I opened up the third by walking Doran. I balked him to second. I had turned to make a pick-off throw to first, and the umpire said I didn't step off the rubber. Worrying about steals interfered with my pitching again. Mark Baily singled and Doran scored.

Ryan came up. I knew he would be bunting. He squared around, I threw the fastball right where I wanted it—up and in—and charged the plate like I was supposed to, but he bunted a little bloop that went right over my glove, for a hit.

Kevin Bass laid down a perfect drag bunt toward third. By the time Hubie Brooks picked it up, it was too late to make a throw.

I had never really caught my breath. I was tired and trying to push myself. A couple of little mistakes and suddenly everything was going the wrong way. One minute I was cruising, next minute I was crashing. I looked around the bases and there were bodies all over the place. I had my good fastball, but I couldn't get good velocity on my curveball.

Another single made it 3–1. I struck out Cruz, which was a big out, but I just couldn't get stuff going back my way. I gave up another walk to load the bases again. Two more singles made it 6–1.

Davey came and took me out. They got two more runs off Craig Swan, which were charged to me. So in two and a third innings I gave up six hits and eight runs. That last inning was my worst inning ever.

Ryan pitched a complete game and they beat us 10–1. The big strikeout confrontation amounted to four for me and seven for him.

Going through that taught me a lot. I really knew now that you had to relax and pitch your game and worry about the hitters instead of who your opposing pitcher was. And that helped me later when I pitched against Soto and Valenzuela and Honeycutt and those guys.

It was good I learned that lesson when I did, because my next start would be against Valenzuela and the Dodgers, in L.A.

We finished up the home stand with a loss to the Reds

and a split with the Braves. Then there were a couple of pitching changes. Tim Leary was switched from a starter to a reliever, and Ed Lynch became a starter. Lynch had wanted to be a starter from the beginning, but they had preferred to have him come from the bullpen and bring Leary along as a starter. Now Leary didn't like being sent to the bullpen too much; he had hoped to have more of a chance as a starter.

The Mets released Craig Swan and brought Tom Gorman again from Tidewater. Swan was the first player to be dropped, and it was a strange feeling for me. Sometimes you might hear a rumor or something before a thing like that happens, but about Swan I never knew anything. You come to the ballpark and you see his locker empty, and then word gets around that he got released. I didn't see him at all, he was just gone.

You miss somebody like that for a while, then you get over it. About a week later I heard that Swan had been picked up by the California Angels. The idea of somebody being released didn't scare me at that time, because of my age. But if I had been thirty it might have brought some fear to me, knowing that as time goes along you might go, too.

I had never been in California before, and the area around the Dodger ballpark looked a little bit like home, Tampa. The weather was like home, too. But the stadium was big, and they had something like 50,000 fans in there, and they were Valenzuela's hometown fans, not mine. This was only five days after the Nolan Ryan game, and they were giving this a big buildup again, me against Valenzuela. But I was a little more relaxed because I knew how to handle it better by then. And by playing away from your own home crowd, you're not so worried about getting booed or letting your own fans down.

I had watched Valenzuela a lot on TV. Ryan is more of

an overpowering pitcher, but one of the things that makes him so effective is that he has a very sharp curveball—maybe it breaks a little sharper than mine, but I think I can get mine over for strikes more often. If Ryan's curve isn't working, he's in trouble. Valenzuela's more of a finesse pitcher, and he has more pitches than Ryan, four or five pitches he can go with in certain situations.

But learning from the Ryan game, I was determined not to worry about Valenzuela, except that again I figured it'd be a low-scoring game.

Early in the game, I was getting them out and getting some strikeouts, but again I didn't have my good curveball. That scared me a little, because I thought about my last start against Ryan when I didn't have the curveball. But I kept showing it to the hitters off and on until it came.

We got a run in the second. With us ahead 1–0, the Dodgers loaded the bases with two out in the fourth, and Rick Monday, a good left-handed hitter, was up. A few days before, Stottlemyre had been working with me on some pitches, and we had talked about how when I hold the fastball with the seams it tails away a little from a left-handed hitter. When I hold it across the seams, it has a little more hop, but it tails in to a left-hander. Stottlemyre told me that in key situations I might want to change grips and give the hitter a little movement that he hasn't seen.

I threw Monday two fastballs that I had gripped across the seams, and he fouled them off. Then I thought about what Stottlemyre had said. I decided to grip the ball with the seams for the next pitch. We have a way I can signal to the catcher if I'm going to change the grip on the fastball, and now I gave that signal to Mike Fitzgerald, so he'd know what was coming. He set up on the outside of the plate. I threw, the ball tailed away, and Monday didn't know what was going on. It got him looking, to retire the side and strand the runners.

We got another run in the top of the sixth. Then in the Dodger half, Steve Sax singled. Making a pick-off move to first, I got called again for a balk.

I didn't get called for balks in the minors, yet sometimes with the Mets I got called even when I was sure I stepped off the rubber. I thought maybe the umpires might be picking on me a little because I was a rookie, to see how I'd react. Strawberry and Hernandez had told me about that possibility, and said that no matter what call they made, not to say anything or stare at them or try to show them up, because if they were testing you, and you respected their calls, they might loosen up on you. So I never said or did anything. I still had to worry about steals, though. Along with my high leg kick I had a tendency to swing the leg back toward second before coming to the plate, and a lot of people were running on me.

Sax went to third on an infield out, so I had a runner on third with one out, and Whitfield and Pedro Guerrero coming up. But my curveball was working now, and that made everything more effective.

Whitfield had got a hit off my curveball earlier, so I went after him with hard stuff and struck him out swinging. Guerrero was a power hitter. I pitched him hard and in where he couldn't do too much with it and struck him out too.

That gave me some confidence, because I felt once I got out of that jam, the rest of the game I could just cruise on through.

Usually I get tougher as the game goes on. If you don't get me by the third or fourth inning, I find my rhythm and get everything flowing my way. It's always been that way for me. I try to come out and pitch four or five strong innings. I don't really get loose until then. After five, the next two innings I'll try to spot the ball more, shooting for seven successful innings. Once I get that, with just a couple of innings left I go with everything I've got left in me, air out every pitch I've got, let everything pour out. Because those are the last pitches, I haven't got anything to worry about after that. If I start getting tired they're going to bring somebody in for me anyway, so I let it all out.

That's what I did with the Dodgers. I really started striking batters out. I struck out 8 of the last 12 batters. In the ninth, I got out there and just sort of exploded, and struck out the side to end the game.

So on my first visit to Los Angeles, I got my first complete game, my first shutout, on a four-hitter, and my top strikeout total up to that time—11—and got us back in first place by half a game over the Cubs.

I also got my first major league hit, off Fernando Valenzuela.

I used to kind of brag about my hitting when I came to the Mets, because I had hit well in high school. I was always a pretty good contact hitter. Even as a pitcher it was important to hit and bunt, because a lot of times late in a ball game if you can't hit, you're gone—they'll pinch-hit for you. If you're a good contact hitter and can bunt the ball, you've got a better chance of staying in the game. That's why a lot of times even between starts I'll go in the batting cage and hit.

I figured one of the reasons I hadn't got any hits so far was because I had never used a wood bat before. We used aluminum bats all through high school, and then I didn't get to hit in the minors because we had the Designated Hitter rule. So I teased the Mets players about how good a hitter I used to be in high school. And they would say, "When you gonna show us?" A lot of pitchers brag about how they can hit, and I hadn't even been on base yet. I would say that if I could take batting practice every day and play every day I could hit .300 in the big leagues. Nobody believed me. Mookie Wilson bet me a dinner that I wouldn't even hit .200 that year.

Sometimes I teased Davey Johnson about it too. When he'd be ready to send up a pinch hitter for somebody, I'd put on my helmet and say, "Davey, I'm ready." I love to hit.

In the third inning, my first at-bat against Valenzuela, I got my first hit. I wanted to see how he was throwing, so I took the first pitch, a fastball right down the middle. I should have swung at that one because it was a good pitch to hit. He came back with a slider, and I should have swung at that too, but I took it for strike two. Now he had me where he wanted me, and I just had to go for it. Next pitch was a screwball, one of his best pitches, and I just kind of stuck the bat out and got a hit over the shortstop's head.

When I got to first base, Bill Robinson, the hitting coach who was coaching first base that game, was chuckling. He said I made it look easy by taking the easy pitches and then hitting the tough one like there was nothing to it. But he congratulated me, and got the ball I had hit back for me so I could have it.

My first hit brought my batting average up to .071, far away from .200 so far.

In the eighth, I had a chance to prove how well I could bunt. With us ahead 2–0, we had two runners on, and one out. Valenzuela walked Fitzgerald to load the bases and pitch to me. With Strawberry on third, they called for a suicide squeeze.

But Strawberry left a little early, and Valenzuela threw it outside, more like a pitchout, and I couldn't reach it to bunt. So I missed it, and the catcher tagged Strawberry out. And then I ended up striking out besides.

As far as strikeouts were concerned, Valenzuela got 8 to my 11. I struck him out twice, he struck me out once. But that one more time I struck him out tied me with him for second behind Ryan, with 51 each.

Beating Valenzuela after the Ryan loss made me feel like I was back on the track again.

We split two more games with the Dodgers and then split two with the San Francisco Giants, so we were tied for first with the Cubs when we went into San Diego, where I would pitch against the Padres.

Jerry Martin, who had been a catcher and outfielder with Kansas City the year before, joined the team, and I wondered how that was going to go. That year he had gotten in trouble on cocaine charges, along with Willie Wilson and Willie Aikens and Vida Blue, and spent some time in jail. I thought we might have a team meeting on him, but we didn't. I think he handled himself pretty well, and people treated him normally. Maybe he thought the fans looked at him a little differently, but the players respected him as though nothing had ever happened, and I was glad to see that. I got to know him pretty well. We used to ride to the ballpark together sometimes back in New York.

Drugs are one thing I've thought about and always stayed away from. Back in high school, sometimes in the restrooms there'd be some drug dealing going on. It didn't really bother me. It was just that a lot of times you'd go in there and not really feel comfortable because you knew if a teacher came in they'd get busted, and if you were in there you were going to get taken too. But I never got involved with anything. When I was on the high school baseball team, a couple of guys I knew would say, "Try this before the game, you'll feel a lot better and more relaxed, and no telling what kind of progress you'll come up with." And I just said, "Naw," or "Maybe later," something like that just to get them off me and stop asking me about it. It was marijuana and Quaaludes mostly. I never saw any cocaine.

With the Mets, I never heard anybody say anybody else was using drugs, never saw anything. I heard about it going on in some team clubhouses, but not in ours. Nobody on the team ever offered me anything, and I never heard of it being offered. Strawberry had warned me to be aware of the matter, about people outside the team, because last year it happened to him a couple of times on the road. Somebody'd call his room and say he was their idol, and they had some cocaine or marijuana and they'd love to come up and have a good time with him. So he wanted me to know that could happen and be aware of it. But nobody ever approached me.

At San Diego, something happened before I even pitched. Maybe it was an omen. The Padres' manager, Dick Williams, came out and asked the umpire to make me take off the gold chain I was wearing around my neck. It was just a rope chain a girlfriend had given me the year before when I was pitching in Lynchburg, and after that I won something like 15 in a row, so since then I thought I'd better stick with the chain when I pitched.

Davey had told us that a lot of managers and players had been complaining about hitters being distracted by gold chains, and there was a rule about it. Davey said we could wear them, but if they told us to take them off we had to take them off. The umpire told me to take it off and I did. I left it off a couple of games, then I saw some pitchers go back to wearing them, so I wore mine again, and nobody said anything about it.

I held the Padres for three innings, and their pitcher, Ed Whitson, held us too. Then I started making some mistake pitches, throwing the wrong pitches in certain situations, guessing and trying to trick the hitters instead of going right at them, and I ended up getting hurt.

In the fourth, Tony Gwynn pulled a fastball pretty well and hit it up the alley in right center for a triple, the first I had given up all year. Then Bobby Brown looped a ball over short that he got a double on, which scored a run. I struck out Steve Garvey. A couple of walks loaded the bases. I struck out Graig Nettles. Then Gary Templeton singled up the middle. Finally I struck out Whitson. But they got three runs.

They got another run in the fourth, before Davey took me out with two outs. It wasn't really a bad game for me because the only hard hit of the five was the triple, and I had eight strikeouts. They beat us 5–4.

That made my record three and three. I thought about last year when I was 3 and 3 at one time also with Lynch-burg, and about that time I went on to win 15 in a row. I had just run into one bad inning, that's all, so I figured next game I'm just going to try and pick up and get wins the way I did last year.

But the Cubs had also won that night, so we were behind them by a game. The Padres beat us again 8–3. Ed Lynch pitched four perfect innings, but then the Padres got three home runs. It was our fourth loss in five games.

We went home and lost two to the Giants. The Cubs and Phillies kept winning, and by the time the Dodgers came in for my next start, we were in third place, four and a half behind the Cubs and three behind the Phillies. We needed to turn things around.

I was facing Rick Honeycutt, who was 6–1 at the time, and I had heard a lot about how good he was. And also I knew that the Dodger hitters would be all pumped up and out to get me because I had shut them out last time.

Basically, I would go at them the same way this time, the same selection of pitches.

I wanted to make sure Sax didn't get on base because he'd try to steal. I didn't want anybody on base when Guerrero came up, because he's a real power hitter. I had been successful against Guerrero in L.A., and had struck him out. If I had to, I could pitch around him to get to weaker hitters.

That was my plan, and things went pretty well. I was pitching one of my better games, shut them out for 8 innings, with 14 strikeouts, which was my high for the majors so far. Foster got a home run in the second and we got another run in the third, so we were up 2–0 going into the ninth.

Top of the ninth I was just going to explode and let everything out the way I did in L.A. Guerrero was the first batter up in the ninth, and I had already struck him out twice. He took a fastball for a strike, then fouled off a curveball. He took two fastballs for balls.

With the count 2–2, I wanted to throw the curve, but Fitzgerald put down fastball. I shook him off. Hitters don't always know when I'm shaking off the sign. If my catcher puts down his fist and wiggles it, he means I should just shake my head. Sometimes we want the hitter to start wondering, thinking Fitzgerald has called for a pitch that I don't want. Like, if I throw a fastball for a strike and then a curveball for a ball, the batter's thinking the catcher will signal fastball. But if I seem to shake off the sign, he doesn't know what to think, and it messes him up.

But this time, I really wanted to throw the curve, so I shook off the sign. Fitzgerald put down fastball again; he really wanted that pitch. So I went ahead and threw it. But I overthrew and got the ball up—right in his warehouse where he likes it—and he pulled it over the fence in left center.

It was the first home run off me in the majors. But it was only the third hit off me in the game, it was the only mistake pitch I had made, and it was the first run off me in 17 innings.

But I was kind of shocked, because now it was 2–1 with no outs, and the Dodgers were back in it.

When Guerrero was going around the bases, I just wanted the ball from the umpire, to get going on the next hitter. I figured Guerrero's going to get his home runs regardless, with his power. And usually when things start going the wrong way for me, I don't want to wait, I want the ball so I can get right back to work.

But Davey came out of the dugout, to the mound. He said, "You threw a great game, and I know you'd like to finish it, but we're gonna go with Orosco."

I don't always want to go the whole game. Sometimes if we've got a lot of runs or if I'm not concentrating so much, around the seventh inning I'd rather come out. I don't want to take a chance on hurting the team. Basically, Davey tells us to shoot for seven good innings, then he can go to the bullpen for the last two.

In this case, here in the ninth I still felt great and wouldn't have minded finishing it. But they had some left-handed hitters coming up, and Davey could bring in Orosco, who is one of the best left-handed pitchers in the league. So I approved of that move pretty much.

When I came off the mound, the fans gave me a standing ovation. That was the first time that had happened to me. Then when Davey came off, they started booing him. That was the first time I had heard that, too. The thing was, they wanted the strikeouts, but we wanted the win, and Orosco held them for us.

At the end of May, by the time we had split with the

Dodgers and lost to the Padres and dropped the first game to the Cardinals, we were just a game over .500 and tied with Montreal for third place.

Strawberry had gone into a slump at the plate. He was hitting the ball, but everything he hit was right at somebody. But he was okay, he knew it was just one of those things you go through. He knew what to do to be successful, so it was just a matter of time until he got it going again.

Hubie Brooks was on a hitting streak. He had tied the Mets record of getting a hit in 23 straight games, which was set in 1970 by Cleon Jones and tied in 1975 by Mike Vail. Hubie was a fun-type guy, probably the most fun on the team, with horsing around. I had met him in spring training the year before when I was with Lynchburg, and we always talked and laughed a lot. He kept me right. When I first got to New York, he showed me around and introduced me to people, and on the road he showed me places to hang out and places not to go.

This year, before spring training started, Davey had said Hubie was going to be one of our better players. Now this outstanding hitting streak was going on. It was different from when a pitcher's got a no-hitter going, and everybody on the team will keep quiet about it, because with a hitting streak the press is talking to him about it every day after the game. So we were all talking about it. And he was unbelievable, because there must have been at least eight games where he'd be up with his last at-bat, and the pressure was really on him, and he'd come through with a hit. Everybody was pulling for him and cheering him on. I know I got really involved in that.

We had started out the season with a four-man pitching rotation because we had so many days off in April. Then in May we went to five. A regular four-day rotation would be a little tough for me. I tend to start tightening up unless I have four days rest. A five-man rotation makes me most comfortable. Now the rotation was me, Darling, Terrell, Torrez, and Lynch.

A couple of days of rain gave me some extra rest. I went against the Cardinals on June 1 with six days of rest instead of four. I like the rest, but sometimes extra days of it actually leave me feeling too strong, and I tend to overthrow. I was going against Joaquin Andujar, who was 8–4 at the time. I had watched him throw the ball in spring training and I knew he threw really hard. Plus, hitters said he was tough, and when I hear hitters say that it kind of worries me. I knew I was going to have to hold them down.

The Cardinals don't have many power hitters, but they have a lot of good contact hitters and a lot of speed. So I had to keep them off the bases so they couldn't steal. If they got runners in scoring position, I would have to bear down more and go up and in or down and away with fastballs. The Cardinals are the kind of team you want to throw more fastballs to than off-speed pitches, because they want the curveball where they can hound it, beat it into the ground, and use their speed to get infield hits.

It was a game we needed to win, because we were starting to slip in the standings.

For the first three innings people were getting on base off me—hits, walks. I had forgotten about following through and paying attention to my mechanics because I was worrying about their speed. And they were knocking the ball around and stealing bases. I kind of lost confidence in myself, to where I thought: I'm just going to throw without thinking too much about it, because they're going to hit it anyway. At the time I wasn't striking anybody out, and it seemed as if everything I threw they were hitting somewhere.

They didn't score until the third. Ozzie Smith singled

and stole second. Then he stole third, and he got such a good jump on me that Fitzgerald didn't even bother throwing. That was why my plan had been not to let them get on base. But they were getting on and they were running. That bothered me especially because it was a close game. Andujar was shutting us out. A sacrifice fly scored Smith, and they were ahead 1–0.

I had to walk off the mound and talk to myself. I was pitching too fast. Most of the time when I do that it's because I'm in trouble, giving up some hits or walks, and I get impatient, just start throwing without thinking. Then I have to stop and tell myself to get my mind on the game, concentrate on making my best pitches, and mix them up. Sometimes when I get in a state like that I have a tendency to stay with just one pitch.

So it was the third inning before I realized what I was doing, but when I stepped off the mound I got myself together. Once I did that, I retired seven or eight batters in a row, mixing pitches up and throwing really well.

We got a run in the fourth to tie it. In the seventh, we got a couple of men on base with one out, and Davey sent Rusty Staub up to pinch-hit for me. Staub popped up and we didn't score. I left the game 1–1, gave up four hits, and had seven strikeouts. I was throwing the ball well by then, but the Cards had stolen six bases off me, and I wasn't happy about that.

Also, we lost. Jesse Orosco, whom we usually could count on in relief, gave up four runs in the ninth. He got the loss. I got a no-decision. That dropped us into fourth place, four games behind the Cubs. With a record of 22–22, we were down at .500 for the first time since we had split the first two games of the season in Cincinnati.

One thing I was happy about, though, was that Hubie got a hit. With that, he set a new Mets record by hitting in 24 straight games. The next day he went hitless, and the streak was ended. We congratulated him afterward and told him to just pick it up again tomorrow. He was happy he had the record, and we were all happy we got a win, 5–2.

But the Cards closed out our home stand the day after that, beating us 1–0. Mike Torrez was the victim because we couldn't get him any runs. That made him 0–5 on the year, and he was a little down and worried about his future.

We were all aware of his record. We tried not to treat him as though anything was wrong, just talked to him normally. Players were really trying to be helpful. In a situation like that, coaches have us doing things to help a pitcher who's struggling. If it's going to be a close play, we won't take any chances running for the extra base, just hope we can bring runners in with hits. And rather than take a chance on hitting into a double play, coaches might call for a bunt. Anything to get on base and get some runs and help the pitcher out.

Mike didn't really know why things weren't going his way. It's tough to lose your fifth straight game 1–0. He thought maybe he wasn't being left in games long enough, not being given enough chance. In that game, he pitched only six innings before Davey took him out. We could have really helped him out if we'd have gotten a couple of runs for him here and there.

But he was pretty down. He said, "They're gonna release me, I know my time is coming to an end." We just told him to hang with it, things were bound to change for the better sooner or later.

We went into Pittsburgh, and Darling and Terrell got wins over the Pirates. That gave Darling a record of 4–3. Terrell shut them out, and that was his first win after four straight losses, bringing his record to 4–5.

My record was 4–3 before my start in Pittsburgh, which

is not all that great. But I had been throwing the ball well lately and getting to know the hitters. The year before, I started out the same way with not too great a record in the beginning, and things turned around. I wasn't really getting many runs scored for me. But I also knew that when you're throwing a game against a tough pitcher for the other side, you will try to be tougher also because you're not going to score many runs. Just as I tried to be tougher in that situation, I had to think about how maybe other pitchers were being tougher when they had to go against me.

After a couple of games when I started getting a lot of strikeouts, and my off-speed pitches were coming well, which made my fastball more effective, I figured things were going to turn my way. I started to think my year could turn out pretty well.

So now we had won a couple of games in Pittsburgh. I was pitching the third game, and it was important to keep the momentum going.

Rick Rhoden was going against me, and it was another one of those tough games. We were shutting each other out until we got a run in the sixth and went ahead 1–0. I wasn't striking out a lot of batters but I was putting them down pretty well.

When I came off the mound after the seventh inning and was walking toward the dugout, a fan sitting behind our dugout hollered, "You ain't gonna get a no-hitter, Gooden!"

I had been concentrating so much on making my pitches that I hadn't thought about anything else. Nobody had mentioned anything to me. I knew that the Pirates had a couple of guys who tried to rile me by stepping out of the box a few times just when I was ready to start my windup. Tony Pena did it a few times, and Jason Thompson. I didn't think that was necessary, because I'm not a fast-working pitcher like Steve Carlton or Mike Williams or those guys, where maybe a batter needs to step out to slow things down and get himself together. I'm mostly easygoing and take my time. But they kept doing it. So I guess they were trying to break my rhythm and mess up my concentration. Usually that makes me want to concentrate even more. So it didn't bother me, and I was getting them out.

Now this fan hollered about a no-hitter. Ed Lynch, who would start the next game, was charting my pitches, but I didn't want to ask him about it. So I looked out at the scoreboard and saw it. At first it was kind of hard to believe, and I didn't know if the scoreboard had made a mistake. But then I realized it was true, nobody had got a hit.

Coming this far, I started to smell a no-hitter, and I just figured I had it in the bag right now because I was making great pitches. Now I would just bear down and let everything go the last couple of innings.

The first batter in the eighth was Doug Frobel, an outfielder who didn't have much of an average and who I wasn't having any trouble with at all. Late in the game like that with me throwing so well I figured I had a sure out.

First pitch, a fastball in on his hands, Frobel broke his bat hitting it. A piece of the bat went down toward first and the ball blooped over short. Gardenhire almost made a great play on it, but it fell in for a hit.

A hit like that to break up a no-hitter kind of hurts. Hernandez came over to me right away and said, "Hey, don't worry about it. Just go after the next hitter and keep the shutout. Show me something right here, that you can be strong enough to finish up the game." I said, "Okay."

I walked off the mound and rubbed up the ball and

said to myself: Well, there goes the no-hitter. Maybe I'll get one later on in my career, so just forget about it and get the win. I just had to make up my mind to go after them.

The next hitter, Dale Berra, I knew would be bunting, and when he did, I charged the ball and threw to second to force Frobel. They put in a pinch runner for Berra, and he stole second.

Then they sent up a pinch hitter, Distefano, and he hit a blooper to right. It looked like either Backman or Strawberry could have caught it, but neither one called for the ball, and it dropped between them. Distefano was thrown out trying to stretch it to a double, but the run scored and tied it up.

Stottlemyre came out to talk to me and make sure everything was okay. He said, "You're throwing the ball well, and they only got a couple of cheap hits, so go right at 'em."

They let me stay in. I wasn't surprised. I didn't think they would take me out at that time. I didn't think Davey was worried. I think he wanted to give me a couple more hitters and see how I would react to the situation.

I struck out Wynn to end the inning.

In the ninth, I walked Lee Mazzilli. He stole second and went to third on a groundout. Then Jason Thompson hit a fly to center. Mazzilli tagged up at third. I ran down behind the plate to back up Fitzgerald for the throw. Mookie caught it and Mazzilli took off for the plate. Mookie threw, and right away I saw it wasn't going to be close. Mazzilli scored, the game was over. I had lost it.

I stomped into the dugout swearing to myself and threw my glove down. Lost the no-hitter, lost the shutout, lost the game.

Then I heard them hollering, "Appeal it! Appeal it!"

Davey was shouting and pointing, and Bobby Valentine was shouting. Fitzgerald threw the ball to Hubie Brooks at third, Hubie stepped on the bag, and the umpire called Mazzilli out. Mazzilli had left third too early. I didn't see him leave early, I was just watching the throw. And I thought we had lost the game. It was a real gutsy call by the umpire, Doug Harvey. It was just unbelievable.

So we went into extra innings. Doug Sisk relieved me for a couple of innings, then Tom Gorman got the win when we scored in the thirteenth on a wild pitch.

I had pitched nine innings and allowed two hits, but I got another no-decision. That was my third no-decision so far this season, and in each one of those I had given up just one run.

After the game, the press told me that if I had gotten that no-hitter I would have been the first Met in history to pitch a no-hitter, and also that I would have been the youngest man ever to pitch a no-hitter in the major leagues. I didn't know if that was true or not, but it kind of hurt to hear it, and to know that I had come that close and still missed out on those records. The press also told me that with my 7 strikeouts I had taken the National League lead with 87, two more than Nolan Ryan. That was pretty unbelievable to hear.

We went up to Montreal and took three games. Ed Lynch ran his record to 6-1, Ron Darling went to 5-3, and Mike Torrez finally got his first win. Suddenly we had won six straight and were right back in there challenging for first place.

We came back to Shea for three games with the Pirates, and I pitched the first one. I knew their hitters pretty well now, since my near no-hitter the week before, and we would be going against Rick Rhoden again, the same pitcher.

Dwight displays a classic pitching style. Here he launches into his characteristic high kick. (*Photo:* New York Mets)

Dwight uncoils, his face a study in concentration and determination. (*Photo:* New York Mets)

Dwight's fastball nears the plate at over 90 m.p.h. (*Photo:* New York Mets)

Dwight's eyes are locked on the ball and batter as he follows through. (*Photo:* New York Mets)

Battery mate Mike Fitzgerald consults with Dwight on pitching strategy.
(*Photo:* Ira N. Golden)

Veteran first baseman Keith Hernandez offers Dwight some words of encouragement. (*Photo:* Ira N. Golden)

The old king meets the new: Dwight and all-time strikeout leader Nolan Ryan. (*Photo:* New York Mets)

Met All-Stars (*left to right*) Darryl Strawberry, Dwight Gooden, Jesse Orosco, and Keith Hernandez congratulate each other on their selection to the 1984 NL All-Star Team. (*Photo:* UPI/Bettmann Archive)

From 13 Inches To 43 Feet

That Strikeout by Dwight Gooden passes Grover Cleveland Alexander's N.L. Rookie "K" Record of 227 set in 1911 Congratulations!

The message board tells the tale of Dwight's unstoppable march toward the all-time strikeout record for a rookie. (*Photo:* New York Mets)

From 13 Inches To 43 Feet

That was Dwight's 246 "K" which breaks the All-Time Rookie Major League "K" mark set by Herb Score in 1955 (245 K's)

Loyal fans in the K Korner kept a running count of Dwight's strikeouts. (*Photo:* New York Mets)

Pittsburgh Pirate Marvell Wynne goes down swinging for the record breaker. (*Photo:* New York Mets)

For the first five innings I just couldn't get into a rhythm. I was really tight. It was like trying to do some work on a full stomach. My fastball wasn't really sharp. One of the things I learned that year was that if one pitch isn't working you go to another pitch until the first one comes back. And I learned that even if you don't have your best stuff, you can still hang in there and win. That's when you become more of a pitcher.

I don't always have my real good movement on the fastball. I tell the catcher, when my ball doesn't have good movement, let me know. Sometimes I can tell just by my arm movement or by the way the batters react. But sometimes the catcher can tell better than I whether the ball's moving. When it's not, that's when I start going with location more instead of just going right at the hitters. I might change speeds, take a little off or put a little more on. When I've got my good fastball, I keep the speed about the same—except toward the end of the game when I might air it out a little.

Here against the Pirates, I didn't have my best stuff and had to go with locations more. Fortunately, Hubie Brooks homered in the second and Hernandez hit a two-run homer in the sixth, so I had three runs behind me. They were not getting many hits off me, just three in the first seven innings, but they were hitting the ball pretty hard, some long fly balls.

As the game went on, I started finding myself and getting in the groove. At one point, I struck out five in a row—the last hitter in the sixth, the side in the seventh, and the first hitter in the eighth. Fans were hanging out the red "K" signs from the railing of the upper deck behind third base.

With one out in the eighth, they got three singles and a run. Davey came out to the mound. He asked me if I was all right. I told him the truth. It was real hot and I was sweating a lot like I always do, and I couldn't catch my breath for some reason—I guess because I had a slight cold starting up. If I could have gone off and gotten a drink of water I would've been okay. I told Davey I was out of breath and my mouth felt like a cotton ball. I wanted to come out.

He brought in Orosco, and Jesse shut them out the rest of the way to save me the win, 3–1.

Strawberry was really in a slump. His average had dropped nearly a hundred points in the last five or six weeks, and he went to Davey and suggested he be benched for a while.

Being Rookie of the Year for the year before, he was feeling a lot of pressure to do more than he was doing, but really, he was just in the kind of slump anybody can go through. He was trying too hard to come out of it, instead of going back to basics. He thought he was messing up the team, so he just wanted a couple days off to get himself together.

We were hanging out quite a bit around then. Off the field, he was fine. But in the ballpark he was a little depressed, because the rest of the team was playing well, but he wasn't doing the things that the press had said he would be doing. He would say things like, "I just wish everybody would leave me alone and I'll be all right, just let me do my own thing." I guess by "everybody" he meant the press, because the papers were printing a lot of personal things, like he was having problems with his girlfriend, or maybe he was into stuff he shouldn't be into.

So Davey sat him down for a couple of days.

We split the next two with the Pirates. Ed Lynch shut them out, to make his record 7–1.

Then we went to St. Louis for the first time. Darling

pitched a four-hitter, got his first complete game and his first shutout in beating the Cards 6–0. We were only a half-game behind the Cubs. Then Walt Terrell shut them out 5–0, beating Andujar. Our pitchers had three straight shutouts.

We were in St. Louis right around the trade deadline. There had been a lot of talk that Mike Torrez would get released because of the record he had. Our hotel was right across the street from Busch Stadium. I was walking over to the stadium when I saw Torrez standing there with a lot of reporters around. I figured he had been released.

When I came up, he told me that they gave him his papers. He shook my hand and said I should just keep going and do the things that he had showed me and the things I had been doing. It was a sad time. Especially the expression on his face made me sad. He had helped me with a lot of things because he had been around and knew a lot. I hated to see him leave.

The good part of that time was that because of our last three wins in a row, we were back in first place. I read in the papers that no Mets team had been in first place this late in the season—June 15—since 1976.

I had to pitch the next game in St. Louis to try and keep us there.

CHAPTER 5

June 16–July 7

One thing that I liked right away about the St. Louis
ballpark was the height of the mound. I had already seen
that teams would tailor their mounds to the type of pitchers they had. At Shea, they had guys like me, Darling, and
Terrell, who all throw the ball hard, so we had a nice high
mound. At Houston, where they had Ryan, it's one of the
best mounds in the league for fastball pitchers because
it's so high. And at St. Louis, they had a good high
mound, I guess for Joaquin.

One thing I didn't like about St. Louis was the heat.
People probably think I'm a hot-weather pitcher because
I come from Tampa, but I'm not. In Tampa I might not
have noticed it so much because the high school games
were only seven innings, and I didn't work as hard throwing there as I did in the big leagues. I always pitch in long
sleeves because I like to feel my elbow tucked into a
sleeve, even when it's hot. Busch Stadium is all closed in
except for a roof, like Cincinnati and Pittsburgh. And
that day down there on the artificial turf the temperature
was about 110 degrees, and it was humid.

The Cardinals were a good contact-hitting club, and
their main thing was to hit-and-run a lot and steal and

bunt. My goal was not to let men get on base and have to worry about them trying to steal.

I started out with great stuff, above-average command of my pitches. In the second, Mookie Wilson dropped a fly ball in center field for an error that allowed Darrell Porter to go all the way to third, with no outs. I struck out Steve Braun. But then a groundout allowed Porter to score. It was an unearned run, and it was the first run against our pitchers in 28 innings.

But we also got four runs by the fifth, so we were ahead 4–1. I wasn't getting many strikeouts, but I was getting outs, not walking anybody and not allowing many hits.

With two outs in the seventh, they got a couple of singles, and George Hendrick came up to pinch-hit. I was so hot. Sweat was pouring off me and I had already gone through three or four shirts. It seemed as though I was throwing a lot of pitches and they were fouling off a lot.

I went at Hendrick with hard stuff. He took two strikes, then a curveball low for a ball. Then I came outside with a fastball, and he swung and missed for strike three. I was real happy to walk off the mound.

In the eighth, I got two outs, then they were going to send up a left-handed pinch hitter. Davey came out and called for Orosco. I was happy to come out. Jesse got his thirteenth save, and I got my sixth win to go with three losses.

I think that was my toughest game all year. I got the win, but I was completely drained and exhausted. After the game reporters asked me about where my good stuff was, since I had only gotten three strikeouts. I told them how hot it was and how tired I got, and that I had given up only six hits, and no walks, and no earned runs, and we had won the game. I was satisfied with that, I told them. I don't have to strike everybody out to be successful.

I was more than satisfied. I went into the trainer's room and told Steve Garland that I was excited to know I could be a successful pitcher without striking people out.

Lot of times when I pitch, people figure that if I strike out 10 or more, we're going to win, and if I strike out like 7 or less, we're going to be in trouble. So now I had struck out only three, and saw I could be a real pitcher without that, and I figured that was not bad at all. That was one of the most satisfying things I learned about myself all year.

We got Bruce Berenyi from Cincinnati, to replace Mike Torrez as a starter. I had seen him throw only once, at the start of the season in Cincinnati, and we had beaten him 2–0, but I thought he was a great pitcher. With the stuff he had, it was unbelievable that he had a losing record in Cincinnati—something like 3–7 when he came to the Mets. He got his first start for us in the last game against the Cards, and he lost it, 6–3. So we fell to second place a half-game behind the Phillies.

We came home to face the Phillies for three important games.

It was good being home. I had a nice one-bedroom apartment in Port Washington, Long Island, about 30 minutes from the stadium. It was a new apartment building with four apartments in it. I paid $700 a month, plus more for the furniture. The landlord went out and picked the furniture that I liked and put it in the apartment, and I paid $225 a month for the furniture. That apartment was plenty for me.

A lot of ballplayers lived near me. Strawberry was about two blocks away, Jerry Martin about four or five blocks away. Steve Garland, the trainer, lived near, and so did Fitzgerald.

The neighbors were real nice to me. Everybody in the area—like at the sporting goods store and the grocery store—was friendly. At a nearby pizza place, when I went in after the games and ordered a pizza they'd say, "It's on us." Sometimes after I'd pitched a good game I'd come home and find balloons hanging up and signs saying CONGRATULATIONS, DWIGHT, and some people would come out and clap for me. It was great to know they felt good about me, people I didn't even know. People would come up to me and ask if there was anything they could do for me, ask me to come over for dinner. Once toward the end of the season some neighbors cooked spaghetti —I guess they found out I liked it—so they cooked a big pot of spaghetti and had salad and everything, a special dinner for me.

I didn't go out much during the season. Mainly I stayed home and watched TV or listened to music. During the day I liked to watch movies and soaps on TV. I got into soaps the year before in Lynchburg. I had a roommate who watched them and he got me into watching them. When I came to the Mets, I found that a lot of players watched them all the time and talked about them. So this year I watched soaps a lot (my favorites were "General Hospital" and "All My Children"). I met one of the stars from "The Young and the Restless" one time. I can't recall his name now, but when I was introduced to him, I recognized him. It was kind of strange meeting somebody after you've been watching him on TV—kind of like meeting famous ballplayers after you've watched them.

I love listening to music, especially rock and jazz. My favorite radio station in New York was KISS, 96 FM. I called up one of the managers there and asked him if he could make up some cassettes for me, for my car and my apartment, and he did. In the off-season I like to go out at night for some entertainment or to listen to jazz, but during the season I didn't do too much night stuff. Lots of times I like to be by myself, because I'm a quiet type of person.

After a night game, the first thing I do is call my parents at home, unless it's too late to call, and then I call the next morning. Nights after I pitch I like to get a lot of sleep, then get up the next day at noon or so. Sometimes I go out shopping, like for clothes, just go to the mall and walk around. But mostly I pretty much stay home until it is time to go to the ballpark, around three-thirty or four o'clock.

Eventually I sold my Camaro. Strawberry had been driving a 1984 Mercury that was provided by the Ford Company, and he bought a Mercedes, so he gave me the Mercury to use. He told the Ford people that I was driving it, and they said that was great because they were going to offer me one anyway. They told me if I wanted to use a car of theirs again next season, to just give them a call. Later on I ordered a Mercedes for myself, a silver 380 SE, to have back in Tampa after the season.

I was pretty much getting into a routine as a pitcher. Lots of pitchers, after a start, will put ice on their arm. But if I'm kind of tight after a start, I just get a rubdown, put heat on it, and keep heat on it when I come home. In the minor leagues I learned that if your arm tightens up after a start and you don't put anything on to protect it, it will affect you next time you pitch. In my first year in the Instructional League, George Bamberger and John Cumberland, who was pitching coach at Lynchburg, told me about taking care of my arm and that at night when it's cool I should keep something on my arm to keep it warm.

The day after I pitch I come in a little early and get into

the whirlpool for 10 to 15 minutes. Then I do a lot of running and exercise. Some pitchers like to run distance, like from foul pole to foul pole. Some like to run sprints from foul pole to center field. I like to run all-out sprints. I think that by working hard and quick like that, it helps me more than distance running. I will run maybe 10 to 15 hard sprints, about 60 yards each.

The second day after a start I throw a little on the side, out in the bullpen, for 15 to 20 minutes. Then two days off, and I'll be ready to pitch.

But every day I play a little catch before the game, just to stay loose. Once in a while I'll lift barbells. Sometimes on off days I will do some "power shagging": during early batting practice for players who need special work, before regular batting practice, I will field some balls in the infield or outfield. Pitchers don't have to go to power shagging, but a lot of them go just to get their running out of the way and catch some fly balls or field ground balls just to mess around.

We have a guy who videotapes pitchers and hitters during games. The day after you pitch you can go in and watch yourself on tape. In the minor leagues they didn't have that. It's great seeing yourself on videotape, one of the best things they could have come up with in baseball. That year, 1983, a lot of pitchers on my team didn't see how I could strike out so many hitters, because it didn't look like I was throwing that hard. I don't feel as though I'm throwing that hard either, but some hitters have told me that it's pretty hard to pick up the ball off me until the last instant. I guess that's because I have big hands and hide the ball. When they get ready to swing it's already by them. One guy wrote that I had perfect form and balance. But when I see myself on tape, it's just natural, the way I always threw.

The main thing I picked up on tape this past year is

that often I wasn't following through. I was watching the ball instead. I was standing up, and that causes the ball to be up a lot. After my third or fourth start I picked this up. Now I'm concentrating more on keeping the ball down by following through.

Also, when I get two strikes on the hitter, I often get too tense and try to overthrow my curveball and do too much with it. I start coming from the side more than over the top. Yet when I'm behind in the count, everything's perfect. I could really tell the difference. When your arm is out at three-quarter, instead of coming overhand, the hitter can pick the ball up better. You want the same motion as your fastball. I learned that in high school. In Little League, I threw it more from the side, like a "slurve." Then Coach Reed started to work with me, got me to throw more rotation from the top, and that's when it started to come around. At the beginning of this season, I was scared to throw a curveball when the count was 3–2 or when I was behind in the count. But as the season went on, I began to use the curve more in tough situations, and that forced hitters to think about it more.

I also started watching myself on tape when I had runners on base, studying my pickoff move. Obviously, they were stealing a lot of bases on me. Almost everybody who tried it made it. And then a lot of times I balked. Worrying about steals and balks was interfering with my pitching. I have always had a high leg kick. Back in sandlot and Little League I used to try to lift my leg up like Nolan Ryan. But basically I didn't copy anybody; it just came naturally. Now on the videotape I could see that when I was pitching out of the stretch I wasn't really giving the catcher a chance to throw anybody out.

In the beginning of the season it was brutal. In the second game I pitched the Cubs stole four bases in five tries. A runner could even be standing right on the bag, and when I started to throw, with my high leg kick, he could steal anyway. I saw that I swung my leg back toward second before I came to the plate. And my arms went way up and down. It didn't make any sense. Swinging my leg back didn't really add to my fastball, it was just a habit. So I started working on just bringing my arms up to my chest and stopping, and I swing my leg straight up and go to the plate.

Stottlemyre worked with me on it between starts. The trouble was, when I was throwing on the sidelines, I would feel comfortable. But once the game started I would go back to my old way. At first it bothered me a lot. And the steals were so bad that I think the catchers figured they had only a slight chance of throwing anybody out anyway and didn't try so much. Early in the season, when I was struggling a little bit anyway, the steals bothered me more. But then I figured, well, if they're gonna go, they're gonna go, I can't let it interfere with the rest of my game. I didn't want to get caught up in worrying about them running and forgetting about the batter, and maybe throw a pitch I didn't want to throw, and end up in even bigger trouble.

So I just worked between games on changing my motion and coming quicker to the plate, and in the games tried not to worry about it. As the season went on and I was pitching really well, it didn't matter much. I just got the hitters out.

Sometimes you get bored going to the ballpark every day, over and over. We used to do things to loosen it up, have a change of pace.

At Shea Stadium, after batting practice a lot of players order food sent down from the Diamond Club upstairs. I got a reputation for being a kind of hamburger freak because I made bets with Charlie Samuels, our equipment manager. For instance, for every zero I put on the scoreboard he would buy me a cheeseburger from the Diamond Club. So any time I wanted a cheeseburger, I just told Charlie he had a bet. I would get maybe four cheeseburgers a week that way when we were home. Hubie Brooks started calling me "Wimpy," and the press picked it up.

Strawberry and Ed Lynch kidded around a lot with me. We would throw jokes on each other. For instance, they'd go in the training room and get some Heet, which is rubbing stuff that's real hot when you put it on, and they'd put it in the back of my pants.

Once Strawberry had laid down his hat and glove on the bench in the dugout, and I got some chewing tobacco and put some gum on it and stuck it in the back of his hat. When he put his hat on he got it all stuck in his hair.

Wally Backman and I used to get into a lot of things. I had wanted to get to know him the year before at Tidewater because he and Gardenhire were always having fun and getting into jokes that I wanted to get in on. But back then I was really afraid to talk to those guys. This year we got to know each other well.

One time I came into the locker room after batting practice and Wally had nailed my shoes to the floor. That was because sometime before I had thrown some gum and it got stuck in his hair. Another time we hid his hat and glove when he was at bat in a game, and when he was supposed to go back on the field with the rest of the team he couldn't find them. The whole game was waiting for him until we told him where his hat and glove were.

Before the next game, I was having an interview on the field on live TV, and Wally came up and said, "Excuse me, Dwight, but is this a serious interview?" I said, "Yeah." Then he threw a cup of water on me, right in front of the camera.

Another time in the locker room a lot of the guys got into teasing me about how young I was, and they started squirting shaving cream on me, so I grabbed a can and started squirting back. Steve Garland saw me doing that, and he said, "Gooden, why don't you act your age?" And I said, "I'm trying to."

Lots of times we did that kind of stuff just to loosen up, keep everything light, because it's a long season. Most of the time, it was a happy clubhouse. When things would go bad, guys like Foster and Hernandez and Staub, who've been around, would call us together and keep everybody's head straight.

In the beginning of the season, Davey preferred everybody to be in the dugout during games. Later on, he didn't mind too much about it, so sometimes some other pitchers and I would go down to the bullpen and talk and joke around with the players down there for a couple of innings. But Davey got to where he wanted people on the bench, because too many players were down in the bullpen or in the clubhouse, and that didn't look too good. If you had pitched the day before, then you could sit in the clubhouse for a while and watch the game on TV. But even then Davey preferred that you be in the dugout for a couple of innings.

Lots of times we'd joke around a little on the bench, even with Davey and the coaches. Davey might tease about pinch-hitting me. Or Frank Howard would say if he was hitting against me he'd really be able to take care of his family from all the hits he would get. Or Bobby Valentine would say that I couldn't run or hit or field, so if I couldn't pitch I'd be out of baseball, and that he wouldn't mind coaching another team against me when I was pitching because there's no way I'd win. We used to get on each other and keep each other up.

Often when I'm not pitching I can't sit on the bench

and just watch or talk, I've got to be doing something. I got to the point where I had to have sunflower seeds. If I didn't have sunflower seeds I would just go crazy. I kept a lot of sunflower seeds with me in the dugout so I didn't have to make any extra trips to the clubhouse. Players knew I always had a good supply, and they would get them from me. Many players I've seen will chew tobacco for maybe three innings, then they'll spit it out and put some seeds in for an inning or so, then they'll go back to the chew.

I started on sunflower seeds when I was ten or twelve, following my father's semipro team around. A lot of the players used to chew them, so I wanted to do it too. I tried chewing tobacco the first year I signed for pro ball. But I never could pitch with it, because I'd be concentrating more on not swallowing the juice than on the pitches I had to make. Or I was afraid that if a ball was hit right back to me, or I had to run over and cover a base, I'd probably swallow the juice and spill my guts or something. So when I pitch, I chew gum. Sometimes there's trouble with gum too, not with swallowing it, but with the sweetness. When I first put a stick of gum in my mouth, it's so sweet that it affects my concentration. So I put it in my mouth when I'm in the bullpen warming up, so by the time I go out on the field to pitch, it's not so sweet.

When I'm not pitching, though, I go to the seeds or try a little chewing tobacco.

While we joke around sometimes on the bench, most of the time I pay attention to the games, usually watching the hitters. You try to learn something from every hitter, especially if you're pitching in that series. You want to pick up any little thing about him that can help you in your start.

Or with pitchers, if one of our pitchers throws a certain pitch in a certain situation and the hitter hits it out of the park, I might ask Ron Darling or one of the other pitchers what he would throw in that situation, or he might ask me. Pitchers on the bench might talk it over, when would we throw a certain pitch to a hitter, or go inside or outside or whatever.

The game before the one you pitch, you chart that day's pitcher. You write down every pitch he throws and what the batter does with it. After a pitcher finishes a game, he can look and see what he did, how many pitches, what pitches, how many strikes. And then before you pitch you can go over the charts and scouting reports from the day before.

In my first round of pitching against the various clubs, there were a lot of players I had never heard of or didn't know much about. Before I pitched a game, I would go over the charts by myself. But you can't always tell from that. They might say a guy's a good fastball hitter or off-speed hitter, but it depends on who's pitching. If they say a guy's a good fastball hitter, I can't change my game plan and go to something else just because of that. Plus, they might be talking about an average fastball, like 85–90 miles per hour. A guy might be hitting that, but he might not hit *my* fastball. The reports I like to see are who's hot, who likes to hit-and-run, who likes to swing at the first pitch, which guys are impatient, which part of the field they usually hit the ball to.

After the game I like to look at the charts and see who did what. After you pitch, Stottlemyre will go over the chart with you and ask you things like why you threw a curveball in a certain situation. But basically, when you go out to pitch you're on your own.

Before I pitch, I warm up on the side for 15 minutes. I work up a sweat. Some pitchers use the resin bag a lot to keep their hand dry. But I like my hand to be a little damp, because that way I can feel the threads and get that little extra spin, especially on the curveball. Sometimes I'll put a little resin on the back of my glove hand so I can just touch it. But usually I just wipe my hand on my pants and go from there.

The Phillies came into Shea Stadium and we beat them two out of three to go into first place. I opened up against the Expos, and we had about our most enthusiastic crowd so far. Everything was going great for me. My fastball and curveball were right there, my change-up was the best it's ever been. I was getting strikeouts. Fans were hanging "K" signs up in left field, and I saw the "wave" for the first time. I had heard of that happening in other parks, where fans stand up to make a wave go around the stands, but I had never actually witnessed it. I thought it was great, seeing the fans get into the game, come out and have fun.

We were up 1–0 in the fourth. I got two strikes on Pete Rose, then I tried to go down the middle with a fastball on him, and he slapped one right back off my leg for a hit. Dawson was up. I had had good luck with him every time in the year so far and had struck him out a few times. The first pitch I gave him was a fastball way up. He likes it high, but I thought he wouldn't be close if he swung because it was so far out of the strike zone. But he hit it to right center, out of the ballpark.

We were down 2–1. I led off the fifth. We needed a base runner. A lot of times when I lead off an inning I'll try to bunt for a hit. Bill Gullickson threw a fastball, and I laid a real good bunt down toward third, right along the edge of the grass. When Tim Wallach picked it up he didn't even make a throw.

But it didn't help. In the end, we out-hit them 8–5. I had 11 strikeouts, and I felt like it was one of the best games I had ever thrown. Sometimes you can go out there and have nothing, and you pitch a shutout. Sometimes you have everything and it goes the other way. So we lost, 2–1. It's a funny game sometimes.

We split the next two with the Expos, and Berenyi got his first win for us. But both the Cubs and the Phillies were losing at the same time, so we went down to Philadelphia for a three-game series leading the division by a few percentage points. Darling got his fifth straight win in the first one to give us a full-game lead. Then the Phils shut us out.

Before I pitched the next game there were some stories in the papers about how the Phillies were anxious to hit against me for the first time. Mike Schmidt was quoted as stating that some people were saying I was the best pitcher in baseball. But as good a hitter as he is— one of the people I had been worried about facing when I came to the big leagues—he might have just been trying to set me up. Also, the press was building up a thing about me and Juan Samuel. Samuel, their second baseman, was a good prospect for Rookie of the Year, so they were talking about how we were going to be facing each other for the first time. I wasn't thinking about that so much, but it wasn't like the situation when they built me up against Ryan or Valenzuela, because in this case I did have to worry about his hitting and running—he can hurt you in so many ways.

Brooks and Strawberry were out with wrist injuries, so while we weren't getting many runs before, I figured we'd get even fewer now. Gardenhire moved to third and Rafael Santana came in at short, and Danny Heep took over in right field.

The Phillies were one of the top hitting teams, plus they had speed on the bases. Nobody got any runs the first four innings, but I was having trouble with control and giving up walks. Since it was my first time pitching there and the Phillies were the team we had to beat at the time, I was trying to do a little extra and was overthrowing.

I got by until the fifth. Samuel doubled off a curveball. Jeff Stone tripled with a liner that went right over my head, skidded by Mookie Wilson on the turf, and went to the wall. Von Hayes singled to make it 2–0. Then I walked Mike Schmidt for the second time. I was trying to pitch him too fine because of his power. Hard throwers are usually the ones to give up a lot of home runs. But Foster and Staub had been telling me that power hitters hit most of their home runs not off fastballs but off off-speed pitches that are up. That made me realize that in high school most home runs off me came on off-speed pitches. And later on I found out that this year, of the seven home runs I gave up, only Nettles and Guerrero hit them off fastballs. But pitching to Mike Schmidt that day, I was staying away from the fastball without thinking and trying to avoid his power with curveballs, and I was losing him.

With runners on first and second and no outs, we weren't expecting a steal, so nobody was holding anybody on. Hayes got a good jump on me from second and stole third. At the same time Schmidt stole second. That was six steals in six tries for the Phillies that game. Two more singles made it 5–0.

I finished up that inning, but that was that.

I told the press later that I just had to chalk that one up to experience, which was true. And I said I'd forgotten that game by the time I got to the shower, which was not quite true. I didn't actually put it behind me that quickly. But it didn't follow me home.

Now we were tied with the Cubs for second place, a game behind the Phillies.

We came back to Shea for a long home stand, finishing

up June and the first week of July, taking us all the way to the All-Star break. The balloting for the All-Star team was going on, and Strawberry was leading the votes for National League outfielders.

I was real happy about that. I had first met Strawberry when I signed in 1982. He was in the Instructional League getting ready to go to Venezuela to play winter ball. I didn't like him at first. He was the type of guy who has a lot of confidence in himself and always believes that he's a lot better than anybody else, and there's nothing he can't do. I saw the way he was acting on the field, and I said to my friend Floyd Youmans, "He must think he's God or something." But I didn't really know him. Once I did get to know him, I realized that the way he went about things was just his way of holding his head up and believing in himself. He's more outspoken than I am; he'll say just about anything that's on his mind.

This past year he became a good friend. He helped me in lots of ways, keeping me believing in myself and avoiding some of the problems he had had when he first came up. Back in spring training, he asked me if I thought I was going to make the team. I told him I didn't know, nobody was saying anything to me about it. He said, "If I was the manager you'd be pitching on opening day." Then when I came up, he was telling players, "This is the guy you got to watch out for. Nobody knows where he's coming from, so he's going to be our sneaker. He's going to be our man."

So we started hanging out a lot together. I was always on his side and he was always on mine, whether we were having fun or needed help. And I especially appreciated that he was getting the votes for All-Star, because he had been going through some difficult times with all the pressures during the first half of the season.

Players like him and Foster and Brooks told me that I

should make the All-Star team, but at the time I was only 6–5. Even though I had a good ERA of about 2.80 and a good strikeout ratio, I thought there's no way I'll make the All-Star team with my record. But I figured I had plenty more years to worry about that. Ron Darling was 8–3 and was named National League Pitcher of the Month for June. He had won his last five games in a row, and I thought he had a better shot at it.

We lost the first two to the Atlanta Braves. Foster came up one time with the bases loaded and struck out. The fans booed him. He was in a little slump then, and every time he came to the plate, before the pitcher even threw, the fans would start booing him. Then if he got a hit, they cheered. If he made an out, they booed some more. They were getting on him pretty hard.

I really couldn't understand that. In Philadelphia, there was the same kind of thing with Mike Schmidt—the fans got on him a lot. How can you get on a guy like that who hits maybe 35 home runs and gets over 100 RBI's? Sometimes when the fans started getting on Strawberry, I thought that was unbelievable too.

People said that when Foster had first come over to the Mets, the fans remembered how when he was with the Reds he had hurt the Mets a lot with his bat, so they didn't like him too much at Shea, and off and on they'd been getting on him ever since he'd been here. I guess he was pretty much used to it. I couldn't understand it, though, that they'd boo somebody who's put so much into the game.

And Foster was always very helpful to me. He and Keith Hernandez were the two who probably steadied me the most. They were kind of like father figures to me. Foster was always there if I needed anything or there was anything I wanted to talk about.

Anyway, next time out we beat the Braves in a double-header, and Ron Darling won his sixth straight. In the second game, Foster hit the 300th home run of his career.

I opened against the Astros to begin July. I tried to approach it as just another game, but I was thinking about how they had beat me at Shea in that Nolan Ryan game, so I had something to prove, and I wanted to get back at them.

They got at me right away in the first inning. Bill Doran was the first hitter—the first one I had faced in the major leagues almost three months ago. He hit a 2–1 fastball to the fence in left center field, and then scored on a groundout. We were behind 1–0. We came right back in the second with the same thing—Strawberry tripled and scored on a groundout to tie it up.

I had a little trouble in the fifth and sixth. In the fifth, they had a runner on third with one out, and I struck out Mark Baily and Mike Scott, the pitcher. In the sixth, I walked Dennis Walling. That was the first walk I gave up, and actually I thought I should have struck him out. A couple of curveballs he took I thought were right there, and Fitzgerald said they were strikes. I think that with power pitchers like myself or Ryan, on a count of 2–2 or 3–2, the umpires are looking for a fastball just as the hitters are. And if you throw an outstanding curveball, you surprise them both. The umpires often are either going to guess at it or call it a ball, because they were looking for a fastball and they got fooled also.

After that walk, Jose Cruz hit a double, putting runners on second and third. Then I struck out Jerry Mumphrey.

Wally Backman was hitting well and drove in three runs, so we were up 4–1 going into the ninth. I gave up a couple of singles to put runners on first and third, and Davey came to take me out.

It was one of my better games. The previous two

games, when I got behind hitters I was scared to go right at them, and I was pitching around them. This game I was going right at hitters and had all my pitches. I felt good and wanted to finish it up, and had the confidence I could take care of it, but Davey didn't ask me how I felt. They had some left-handed hitters coming up, and he wanted to bring in Orosco out of the bullpen.

Later I saw that Davey was quoted kind of joking about it, saying that he hadn't asked me how I felt because I would have tried to talk him out of taking me out. A couple of times during the season he would come out late in the game and ask me how I felt, and if I felt good I'd tell him I thought I could finish it up. This time if he'd have asked me I would have asked him to give me at least one more hitter. But then if he'd have said no, I wouldn't have tried to talk him into it. I never argued with Davey.

When he took me out, I got an ovation, and he got booed again the way it had happened a few weeks before. I had 12 strikeouts, and the fans wanted to see more. I didn't feel it was right to boo him. I guess they didn't realize that I had lost my last two starts, and Davey wanted me to have the win. He didn't want to take any chances of me blowing it. But you know how fans are sometimes.

With Orosco, one of the runners scored on an out. But I got the win, 4–2, and that made my record 7–5. We beat the Astros again, 4–3, Berenyi over Ryan. Foster and Hernandez got home runs. Then we had the Fourth of July game, with fireworks and everything, and a sellout crowd. But the Astros scored five runs in the first inning and beat Ed Lynch 10–5.

After that game a limousine came to pick me up because the next morning I was scheduled to be on the "Today" show. They took me into Manhattan to stay at a hotel so I could be at the show early in the morning. That was the only one of those really big interview shows I'd ever been on. I'd been talking to reporters, so I had some experience, but I was still a little nervous. I was afraid Bryant Gumble was going to ask me tough questions about things I didn't know and that I would panic, but he was pretty easy on me and talked to me in a way that made me feel relaxed, so I wasn't afraid of the cameras. He asked me what our chances for the pennant were this year. I told him there was no doubt in my mind that we could win it, or be contenders to the end.

We had the Reds coming in for a big five-game series, our last games before the All-Star break. The Reds were struggling, in next to last place in the NL West, but they had played us tough. I figured I'd have to go against Mario Soto in one of the games, and he was 9–1. Since we were just a game behind the Cubs, how we did against Cincinnati would decide where we were at the All-Star break, halfway through the season.

The day of the first Reds game, the final balloting by fans for the All-Star teams, was announced. We knew who the starting lineups would be because the press had been carrying the voting all along. Strawberry got the most votes for National League outfielder. They said he was the first Met to be voted to the All-Star starting team since Dave Kingman in 1976. The only people in the whole league to get more votes than Strawberry were Steve Garvey of the Padres for first base and Mike Schmidt of the Phillies for third base.

Paul Owens, the Phillies' manager and the manager for the NL All-Stars, added Keith Hernandez to the team. Everybody knew he should be on the team because he was having the best year of any first baseman.

But when Owens named the pitching staff, I couldn't believe it. Along with such veteran stars as Charlie Lea and Joaquin Andujar and Mario Soto and Rich Gossage and Al Holland and Bruce Sutter and our own Jesse Orosco, he picked me.

We had four people on the All-Star team, and I couldn't believe one of them was me. I wasn't even on the team in spring training, and two years ago I was in high school.

The press was all over us because this was the largest number of Mets ever picked for the All-Star team, and they said I was the youngest All-Star ever in the history of the game. I couldn't think of anything to say other than that it was a great honor, that it was unbelievable to go from Class A last year to the All-Star game this year, and that I would do my best if I got a chance to pitch.

In the dugout before the game against the Reds, we were all congratulating each other and feeling on top of the world. I was a little surprised that Ron Darling hadn't been picked, because he was 9–3 and had won six in a row, and that Hubie Brooks was passed by, because he was hitting over .300 and had that hitting-streak record. They were disappointed, but they took it pretty well.

We had to remind ourselves that we still had some ball games to win before the All-Star break, and we had to turn our attention to the Reds. I wasn't pitching for a couple of days, which was lucky, because I needed those days to get my head together.

Strawberry seemed to have his head together already, because he went out and hit a home run in the first inning, then got a double in the eighth, and we beat the Reds behind Walt Terrell, 4–3.

Then we swept them in a double-header, which was our third straight double-header sweep of the season. Darling pitched a four-hitter and won 1–0 for his seventh straight.

We had won seven out of our last eight, and were a

half-game behind the Cubs. It was time for me to go against Soto.

In the paper that day I saw that no other team in the league had scored as few runs as the Mets so far this year. That was a surprise because we were doing pretty well, although I knew our pitchers, including myself, were wishing we could get more runs behind us from time to time. Since we were going against Soto, who was 7–0 against the Mets in his career, I figured we wouldn't get many runs, so I couldn't afford to give up any. I managed to put the All-Star game out of my mind because we were going for first place.

The Reds got a run off me in the third when Duane Walker doubled and Dan Driessen singled him in. Keith Hernandez knew I was a little worried about them getting the lead behind Soto, and he came over from first base and said, "Hey, big guy, don't worry about that run. One run ain't gonna beat us. If you just hold them right there, we're gonna win the ball game."

Our guys jumped on Soto that same inning. I think maybe he was a little rusty coming off a suspension he had gotten for being in a brawl and throwing a ball at somebody. We got two in the third and seven in the fourth, which got rid of Soto.

We ended up getting 18 hits and 14 runs, which they said was the most runs the Mets had scored since 1979. Mookie Wilson was 4-for-4, and he and Strawberry got home runs. Even I had two RBI's, on a sacrifice fly and a groundout. We won 14–4, and the Cubs were losing in San Francisco, so we took over first place.

I didn't pitch a great game because I gave up 10 hits in the 6 innings I pitched. Once I got the big lead, I wasn't concentrating too much. I kind of laid back a little, which a pitcher should never do. But then again I hadn't had many big leads in the big leagues. I did manage to strike out 8, and later reporters told me that I was leading the league with 133 strikeouts.

Then the next day Bruce Berenyi went out and beat the Reds 7–3 on a six-hitter, and we had a five-game sweep and were in first place for the All-Star break. We were playing great ball, hitting and pitching were coming together for just about the first time in the season. In a way, we hated to see the All-Star game come when it did, because we thought it might break our rhythm and momentum.

Jay Horwitz, the director of public relations for the Mets, told me I had been named National League Player of the Week, because I had won two games that week with a 2.51 ERA and 20 strikeouts. It was a great honor to have and I was really thrilled because I had always wanted to be named that, the way Hernandez had been. They give you a certificate and a really nice baseball watch, where the second hand is a little man running around the bases. It was great to get that award just before heading to San Francisco to be in the All-Star game.

CHAPTER 6

July 8–12

They gave each player two tickets, and I took a girlfriend from Tampa with me to San Francisco. We got together with two of my brothers who live near there. I hadn't seen them in quite a while, and we had dinner together. It was great seeing them, but I was pretty nervous about everything.

The day before the game was a workout day. I was really nervous when I got to Candlestick Park for that. There was lots of press around, TV cameras and everything, everybody wanting interviews.

Talking to some of the players made me feel better. Steve Garvey congratulated me on making the team, and said I should stay healthy and that this All-Star game would be just the first of many for me. Mike Schmidt also congratulated me on the year I was having, and said the main thing was just to enjoy being there and have fun. They had been in lots of All-Star games. But for me, going to spring training thinking you're not going to make the team, then making the team, and now being on the All-Star team, being around a lot of players that have meant so much to the game, talking to them, being in the same clubhouse, working out with them—it was all a strange feeling.

By that time I felt I belonged in the big leagues, but the All-Star team was a step higher than being in the big leagues, with all those great players. Everybody treated me fine, but I didn't say too much. In the locker room and on the field, I mainly just walked around, watching everybody, checking everybody out.

Some of the pitchers were shagging balls during batting practice. Fernando Valenzuela asked me how I liked the big leagues. Mario Soto, who has one of the best change-ups in the game, told me that he has a tendency after throwing the change to come back and overthrow the fastball. That was interesting to me, because I had been having that problem sometimes, and here was a real veteran pitcher talking about the same thing.

There was some talk that maybe I would start the game for the National League and Phil Niekro of the Yankees for the American League, because then it'd be the youngest against the oldest. That was just talk, because neither one of us started, but I got to meet Niekro and shake his hand. I used to watch him play on TV a long time ago, and I didn't realize how old he was. It was just amazing that he was forty-six years old and still getting around as well as he was and still throwing that knuckleball that tied everybody up.

Paul Owens said that he was going to start Charlie Lea of Montreal, because he was a veteran pitcher, and I would be the third pitcher after Fernando.

I hadn't pitched before in Candlestick Park, but we had played there against the Giants. Usually they didn't draw too many people. But on All-Star game night it was packed, and it sure looked different. When the game started, I was sitting out in the bullpen talking to Orosco and looking around at the crowd. Jesse had been in the

All-Star game last year, and he had pitched to one batter and struck him out, so he had some experience with how it was. But for me, this looked like the biggest crowd I had ever pitched in front of, the game was on nationwide TV, and I didn't know much at all about the American League hitters. So I had a few butterflies. I was thinking mainly that I just didn't want to mess up.

Valenzuela went in to pitch the third inning, and I watched him pitch and thought about how impressive he was. Owens called down to the bullpen and said Valenzuela would pitch one more inning and then I'd be coming in.

So in the fourth inning I started warming up. I wanted to be real careful to warm up right. The wind was blowing as usual in that park, and I was trying to adjust my pitches to it.

But every pitch Valenzuela threw, I stopped to watch him. He struck out Dave Winfield. Then he struck out Reggie Jackson. Then he struck out George Brett. With the crowd standing up and cheering, I thought: We're ahead 2–1 and I have to go in and follow that performance. I tried to block everything out of my mind except what I had to concentrate on to make my pitches.

Fifth inning, my time to pitch. I hadn't pitched in relief since high school, and never as a pro, so even walking in from the bullpen to the mound in front of that crowd was new to me. I walked slowly and tried to get ready for what I had to do. I talked to myself the whole way. I said: Okay, it's just like any other game. All you do is throw strikes and try not to overthrow.

But it wasn't just like any other game. In a regular game, you try to pace yourself, but in the All-Star game, when I had just two innings to pitch, I wanted to air it out and throw everything I had with everything I had. I wasn't thinking strikeouts, but I wanted to throw strikes, and I didn't want to give up any runs and lose the lead, and I didn't want to do anything bad, like throwing a ball all the way to the backstop.

Gary Carter, the catcher, met me at the mound. He asked me what I wanted to go with. I told him, basically fastballs, go right at them. And with the off-speed pitches he could move in and out for location. It was like we'd been playing together all year. He knew my pitches, what I was likely to use in certain situations, from watching me when we played against the Expos and from hitting against me. He said, "Just throw the ball like you have all year, like you did against me." That helped me some with my nervousness. He went back behind the plate and talked to me from there too, telling me to just throw my pitches, pitch my own game. He kept me pumped up.

I was tense while I was warming up. The first thing I noticed was that the wind was blowing the other way. It had been blowing one way in the bullpen, now it was blowing the other way on the mound. So I had to adjust all my pitches again. Carter kept giving me a low target and talking to me. It took me about 12 pitches to get ready, then it was time to play.

The first hitter was Lance Parrish, catcher for the Tigers. At least I had faced him before in spring training. I just wanted to get the first pitch in.

I got it in—he took a fastball for a strike. When I got the ball back from Carter I was more relaxed. Now I was going to go right at him, and whatever happened would happen. The second pitch was a fastball away, and he took it for a ball. I threw my first curveball, and he took that for ball two. He fouled off a fastball for 2–2.

I decided to try to get him right there. I threw the fastball high, and he went for it and missed, for a strikeout.

That took all the nervousness away. The crowd was really into it, and I had a lot of confidence.

The next hitter was Chet Lemon, also of the Tigers, whom I had struck out a couple of times in spring training. But he was a dangerous hitter. Again, the main thing was to get the first strike and take it from there.

I started him off with a fastball also, right down the middle, and he took it for a strike. It looked like they were taking the first one, probably figuring that I was nervous in my first All-Star game and so I might be wild. Then I came back with a curveball, a great one that dropped right off, and he swung and missed. I teased him with a fastball away, and he took it for a ball. I decided to go with the same pitch I got Parrish with, fastball up high. He swung late for another strikeout.

Then it was Alvin Davis of the Seattle Mariners. I knew that he was a rookie also, so I thought he might be more nervous than I was. He was the first left-handed hitter I had faced in the game, but I decided to go with the same pattern I used to deal with Parrish and Lemon—fastballs, curve, back to fastballs. I gave him two fastballs up and in, out of the strike zone, and he helped me out by swinging at both of them. He took the curveball inside for a ball. Then I went back to the fastball up, and got him swinging.

I had struck out the side—it was unbelievable!—and I had got all three hitters on fastballs out of the strike zone. The crowd really appreciated what I had done, and I found out later that Fernando and I had set an All-Star record by striking out six in a row.

When I walked off the mound, the crowd was standing and cheering, and I was walking on air. Everybody in the dugout shook my hand and gave high fives. And all these players were some of the best players in the game, congratulating me.

But even feeling as high as I felt, I didn't figure I'd go on striking everybody out. I was just excited to have another inning to see what I could do against more All-Star hitters.

The first hitter in the sixth was Lou Whitaker of the Tigers. He had given me trouble in spring training. He was a good contact hitter who wasn't likely to strike out, so I figured he'd put the bat on the ball, and he did. On my second pitch, he grounded to first, to Keith Hernandez. I ran over to cover, and Hernandez tossed me the ball for the out.

Then Eddie Murray of the Orioles hit my first pitch for a pop-up over short, and it dropped in for a hit. He went on to second base because nobody was covering. I guess the second baseman, Ryne Sandberg of the Cubs, was watching the ball just the way I was, hoping it'd be caught.

So I had given up a hit, and had a man on second with one out. I told myself it was time to show what kind of pitcher I was, to be tough and pitch out of it. I worked the count to 2–2 on Cal Ripken of the Orioles. Then he pulled my curveball on the ground down the third base line. Mike Schmidt made a great backhand play and threw him out.

Now I had Dave Winfield. I hadn't ever faced him before, because he hadn't played in the game we had against the Yankees in spring training. He was the American League's leading hitter, the most intimidating hitter I had to face. I couldn't afford to make a mistake with him because I knew he could hit one out. I thought he might be swinging for the fence in this situation because we had the lead and they had a man on base, and also because the All-Star game is a showcase where you might want to show the crowd what kind of power you've got. I didn't care so much if I walked him, because first base was open with two outs. I just didn't want to give him anything he could really tag.

We went at each other pretty hard and pretty long. My first fastball he fouled back. He took my second one away, for a ball. I tried to get him to go for a low curveball in the dirt, but he took it. So now it was two balls and one strike. I came with a fastball; he pulled it good but foul, down the left field line. It was 2–2. Fastball up and in; he fouled it off. I went for the outside corner with a fastball and made it close, but he took it for a ball. It was 3–2.

I figured maybe if I got a curveball over right now, I'd have him. Carter called for the curve, and I threw what I thought was a great one, shin high, dropping away from him. He fouled it off. Carter called curveball again, I threw it to the same location, and he fouled it off again.

I didn't want to back off or give him time. I wanted to stay right after him. I thought maybe I could get him the way I did Parrish and Lemon and Davis, so I went up and in, and he fouled that off. So now I figured he wouldn't be looking for my third 3–2 curveball, and that's what I gave him, and he got out in front of it and flied to left field.

I got out of it with no runs scored. I had pitched two innings in the All-Star game, gave up one hit, struck out three. And I had battled Winfield for what seemed like an hour, and got him. Paul Owens said that was enough, and it was.

After the game, the press was all around, and they asked me how it felt to do what I had done, and as the youngest pitcher ever to play in that game how did I account for the poise I had, and all that. I told them that if you know how to pitch, it doesn't matter how old you are, the job is the same, and that's to get hitters out.

That probably sounded easier than I meant it, the way

I was putting it. But I was sure glad things had gone my way, so I didn't have to stand there explaining to them why I had messed up in the All-Star game my first year in the big leagues. I had never faced so many tough hitters in a row like that, and if I faced any of them again, I hoped it would be in the World Series.

If my season had ended right there at the All-Star break, I would have been pretty satisfied. I was 8–5, with an ERA of 2.84, had struck out 133, and my team was leading the NL East. And then pitching well in the All-Star game, that was about the most exciting and satisfying thing so far in my whole career, something I could always look back on with pride, no matter what happened later.

But the season was only half over, and after all that excitement I had to get back to work and take it a game at a time and help the Mets go all the way.

My whole life had changed. I had learned the ropes in the big leagues, been through some pressure situations, been successful so far. I was getting a lot of media attention, and that was probably the biggest change. People get to know you through the media and they see you as different, because you're a ballplayer. Then the way you approach people gets to be different because they know that you're different.

Media attention started in spring training and got bigger up in New York once I started throwing well. It got really big at the All-Star game. There might be 30 members of the press around you at one time. And in New York it got to be like that sometimes. It got to be there'd be some press people wanting to talk to me not only when I pitched, but every day. You don't feel like talking every day, but it's their job, and it's good for you also. I generally like talking to the press. You get tired of it after a while, but then you get used to it. In your first year, you want to get as much publicity as you possibly can.

After you have had a real bad outing, you may want to go home and forget about it, but I hung around and talked to the press whether I was going good or bad, told them the things they wanted to hear and got it over with. I felt that was the best thing to do, because some people, after they had a bad game, would leave and go home, yet when they had a good game they'd hang around and talk to the press. Sometimes the press noticed that and would write bad stuff about you doing that. I agree with the press on that. If you're going to talk, you should talk no matter how you're doing.

Lots of times they ask you the same questions day after day. But then there may be different reporters, like from papers in other cities, and so you answer the questions.

One of the things they'd always ask about was how I had so much poise, how I stayed calm in tough situations as if I were older, and where all that came from. Lots of people figure that when you're pitching in the big leagues and you're nineteen, if you win a game you're supposed to get all excited and jump around, or if you get hit pretty well you're going to be throwing your glove and getting upset. I guess by my not doing those things, they figured I was acting older. But all it is is that before I take the field I like to set myself a game plan and think about what I'm going to do. And if things don't go my way I'm not going to get all upset. Or if I'm throwing a no-hitter I'm not going to get really excited and show up the other team or anything like that. When I'm on the mound I just do my best not to let anything bother me. I don't get too emotional. Whether things are going bad or great for me, I just try to keep the same attitude, the same expression on my face. I learned those lessons when I was small, and how I act now doesn't seem special to me.

Basically, the press has been pretty easy with me. But sometimes they try to get you to say things you don't want to say, like about personal things or controversy or people who might be giving you trouble on or off the field. I don't really worry about people watching me, judging me as a ballplayer. I'm still young, and I just want to work and get to know the hitters in the league. But Strawberry had warned me about not letting anybody put words in your mouth, because that had happened to him a few times, and then it happened to me that time when they said I called the Cubs hot dogs. So I just tried to be careful to say the things I wanted to say, so I wouldn't be misunderstood or get people down on me for some reason.

Sometimes I liked to get on the road, to get away from the media and relax. Every day, whether I pitched or not, there'd be three or four reporters before the game, three or four after. A couple of times I snuck out, went in the training room to sit back there, or in the eating room to eat. But I never did that after I pitched. Only off-days. After every game I pitched, win or lose, I stayed right there.

It was amazing how things had changed. Early in the season when we were in Houston, Strawberry and Hubie Brooks and I went out to eat at a restaurant, and a guy came over and said, "Don't you play ball?" He recognized Brooks and Strawberry. Hubie pointed at me and said, "He plays too." The guy said, "In the minor leagues?" Hubie said, "No, with the Mets." The guy asked my name and I told him. He said, "I never heard of you. Are you really a ballplayer?"

But now I was getting all this attention and people were asking for my autograph everywhere. Guys seventeen or eighteen would be coming to watch me play and get my autograph, and they would say that when they play ball they pretend they are *me,* and I'm only a year or so older. And older people would say I'm their idol, and I'm only nineteen and just starting out.

I got to meet a few celebrities. I never met the President or Mayor Koch, and I didn't know who some of the celebrities actually were, because I hadn't followed their fields too much. But one I remember best was Magic Johnson, the basketball player with the L.A. Lakers. He came to the clubhouse. I was surprised he knew who I was and the things I was doing, and that somebody like that would talk to me the way he did. He said he admired me. When I used to play basketball in the off-season, I would pretend I was either Dr. J or Magic Johnson. Then to actually meet him and hold a conversation with him, it was like, when am I going to wake up?

I always thought that if I met somebody like that I'd have so many things to say. But once you are actually talking to them you can't really find things to say. Mainly he asked me a lot of questions about New York and how I liked it and how was the fast life and stuff like that.

I didn't care much about the fast life. This past year, both at home and on the road, I didn't go out much. The Mets never had a curfew on the road. I guess they figured everybody was adult, and you know what you've got to do to do your job and stay healthy and be in good condition to play ball. I was real careful to stay in condition. Maybe after a special game that we won, or I won, I'd go out with a couple of players and have a beer or two.

Girls came around sometimes. When I first started, they came during batting practice and asked for your autograph, and they might ask you what you were doing after the game, or if they could show you the town. At the beginning it was just every now and then, but as the season went on and I got to be known a little more, they would come around more often. Sometimes at the hotel they'd call and say they'd been watching you on TV and wanted to get to meet you. Or sometimes you'd be out at a club and they'd recognize you and come over and sit down and have a couple of drinks. They'd ask what your plans were for later, or if they could come up to your room. Usually I'd say something like that I was married and my wife was with me, or "I appreciate you coming over and wanting to get to know me but I'm just going to call it a night."

I never checked any of that out, never took any of them up on it. I just didn't want to take the chance with somebody I didn't know. You just can't trust it. They might think that just because I played baseball and I was a teenager they could take advantage of me, take my money or something like that. And at home in New York, I had a girlfriend there a lot of the time, which was nice.

After a while, road trips started getting kind of old. Especially getting up early. You have to pack and get ready to go after a late game at night. You fly out that night, and next morning get up and go to the ballpark. It got to be pretty tough. And then after the games maybe all you want to do is come back and eat dinner and go to sleep. Sometimes I could sleep on the planes. Especially if I had a bad outing, I'd go to sleep. But if I had a good outing, I'd be up playing cards, laughing and talking.

We flew in chartered planes except to California and Montreal; then we went commercial. If we'd just won a big series, the plane would be loose, and everybody'd have a lot of fun, cracking jokes on each other. Davey got into it sometimes. We might get into silly stuff like a grape fight. A couple of times, after some guys went to sleep food was served, including cake. We'd put the cake in the hand of a guy who was sleeping and tickle his face with a straw, and he'd hit himself in the face with the cake. We got Foster like that once.

Sometimes on the road I'd go out walking around with Steve Garland and do some shopping and look at the buildings. Or a few players might go to a movie or to dinner. In San Diego I went to the zoo with Jesse Orosco.

That was about it for the fast life.

Some companies were starting to get interested in me. I signed my first glove contract with Rawlings when I got drafted in 1982. In the minors, they would give you two gloves a year. But in the big leagues they give you whatever gloves you want. I also signed a contract with Starter, who makes the Mets jackets. They give you jackets and stuff, and you wear them in pictures.

And then shoes. In spring training, Brooks Shoes gave me some baseball shoes to try out—no contract, just try out their shoes. So I started off wearing them. Then when I made the team, all the shoe companies came around to talk to me and have me try out their shoes. Converse, Adidas, Nike, Puma—all the companies. They all offered money except Adidas. Adidas said they would give me all the shoes and merchandise I wanted, but they couldn't give out money.

Basically for me it was a question of what shoe felt the best. I have wide feet. I tried different shoes early in the season, and Nike felt the best. Nike said they would give me merchandise, all the shoes I wanted, would get me promotional work, and give me a money contract. I told Jim Neader, my agent, that I wanted to go with Nike. At All-Star time we worked out a deal.

Nike even put up a billboard of me on a building at Forty-second Street and Eighth Avenue in New York. It was amazing. I felt like I had been playing baseball for about 30 years, with my picture up there.

One thing that really surprised me was that *Sports Illustrated* wanted me to sign with them to do some posters. *Sports Illustrated* always seemed to have Mike Schmidt or Pete Rose or some of those guys on the big posters. Now they wanted me. I signed a contract with them, and they said they would work up the posters for next season.

Then there started to be a lot of requests for appearances—clinics, promotions, car shows, banquets. You would sign autographs for a couple of hours and get around $1,000. Lots of times the Mets set them up for me. I don't do too much that they don't know about. And I didn't do too many appearances. You can make more money doing that if you want to, but you don't want to get too busy and lose your concentration on the season. Sometimes they wanted me to go to sporting goods stores and sign autographs for a couple of hours, and I would turn it down because I didn't want to mess up the things I usually do during the day.

There were some things I did that weren't for pay, but were just good things to do. Strawberry and I usually rode to Shea Stadium together on game days, and one day after the All-Star break he told me he'd be going in earlier because he was going to a baseball clinic for a lot of young players, Little Leaguers and so on. It was a clinic put on by the Mobil company to bring in celebrity ballplayers to demonstrate fundamentals to kids.

I asked Strawberry if I could come along, and he said sure. So we got dressed and went out there and went through the motions for the kids. Bill Robinson, the Mets' hitting coach, was on the mike describing how we did things—the proper way to pitch, hit, field, and so on. I thought it was great. We signed autographs and shook a lot of hands. I knew it meant a lot to the kids, because when I was a kid I used to go out at spring training to watch the Cincinnati Reds, and I never got a chance to meet any players or shake hands or any of that, and I knew what it would have meant to me then.

They meet somebody like Strawberry who was Rookie of the Year, somebody that young who was doing something with his life—that can be a good influence on kids. Seeing kids come up and not be in trouble meant a lot to me. And a clinic like that shows them that there's something to strive for, and gives us a chance to tell them how important their parents are and to stay away from drugs.

Especially after the All-Star break, a lot of agents were calling me or writing letters to me at the ballpark, maybe 10 or 20 of them. They would say they just wanted to meet with me and talk, let me hear what they're doing. But it would boil down to them wanting to represent me, and I told them I already had an agent.

I did meet with a couple of them, just to hear what they had to say. They'd tell you how the business operated, what they could do for you, how they could invest in real estate and the stock market, how much experience they had, how well they knew the Mets' organization. Everybody's going to tell you they can do more. Some of them were on the up and up. But some of them were telling me names of players they represented, and I knew these players were represented by somebody else. That gave me the idea that they were trying to put something over on me.

One guy I talked to represented some pretty good players and he tried to talk me into letting him represent me. When I told him I wanted to stick with the agent I had, he said, "Well, maybe you could hire me just to look over your agent and make sure everything's going right."

When you get to be known, people come at you all over the place trying to offer you deals, hustle all kinds of things. Strawberry told me that in his first year, every day

people came around the clubhouse with different deals
to offer him—they could do this and that for him. He said
it was so much that if he had let it get to him, it would
have affected his concentration.

You just have to avoid that stuff. Your job comes first. I
talked to a lot of veteran players and people who have
been around, and they gave me advice and helped me, so
I knew how to deal with it. I think whether you're nineteen or twenty-five or whatever, you can tell when something's not right.

The main thing is, just watch yourself, watch what
you're doing, take care of yourself.

CHAPTER 7

July 12–August 21

We went back to work on July 12, two days after the All-Star game, went right on the road, and picked up right where we had left off: we took three games from the Braves in Atlanta. By the time I pitched my next start against the Braves, we had won eight in a row, the team's longest winning streak since the 1969 Miracle Mets, and were ahead of the Cubs by half a game.

We were hot and pumped up. My confidence was really high after the All-Star game. But then again I knew that because I had been on the All-Star team, other teams were going to be ready for me.

My parents drove up from Tampa for the game. My younger sister came too, and a couple of cousins who lived in Atlanta. My parents had seen me pitch my first start in Houston, but this was the first time my sister and cousins had come to see me. I think I was trying to impress my family more than I was concentrating on what I had to do. Anyway, nothing seemed to go right.

It was a day game, and I didn't do well in day games all year. It was also hot and was raining off and on, and the mound had a sticky kind of clay in it that made me feel like I was pitching up hill. I was wild early. I couldn't put the ball where I wanted it.

I got the first two hitters, but then I grooved a 2–1 fastball right down the middle to Claudell Washington and he hit it out of the park.

Strawberry tied it up in the second with his twelfth home run. The first man I faced in the second was Chris Chambliss. I gave him a fastball way up and in, right across his eyes, and he tomahawked it over the right field wall. After that, Hernandez told me that Chambliss will look for that one pitch high and inside where he can turn on it. I wish I'd known that going into the game. But even so, considering where that pitch was, I don't know how he could hit that ball so hard. Two homers in two innings.

In the third, I gave up another run on a walk and a double by Washington. In the seventh, I gave up some more walks, and they had the bases loaded with one out and Washington up again. He was hitting me pretty hard. I was pitching him tough this time, and we were thinking double play. He hit a broken-bat dribbler to short, and Rafael Santana charged it and threw home. The ball got there in time, but the runner slid into Fitzgerald and knocked the ball out of his mitt. Before I got them out, Chambliss had singled in another run and we were behind 5–3.

I went out after that inning, and we ended up losing 8–3. I had the strikeouts—10—but the walks hurt me. I gave up six, and that's a lot of walks in seven innings. What with the heat, and me pitching with men on base a lot, I was not very effective. Even without the walks and that play at the plate that opened the door for a couple of runs, I still gave up two home runs.

When you have a winning streak stopped like that, it's important to bounce back right away, and we did that the next day against the Astros in Houston. Sid Fernandez was called up from Tidewater for his first start, and he pitched a strong game. We got 22 hits to win 13–3.

The next stretch was real tough, whether we won or lost. There were lots of close calls and late-inning action. At one point we had five straight one-run ball games, and that takes a lot out of you, especially when you're in a pennant race.

The Astros beat us 3–2. Darling pitched great for eight innings, then Doug Sisk relieved and gave up a two-run homer in the ninth. We beat the Astros the next day 3–1 when Hernandez hit a two-run homer off Nolan Ryan—a real big league homer to straightaway center field. You don't hit too many out in center field in the Astrodome.

Then we went to Cincinnati and lost 9–6 because the Reds got three unearned runs for Soto, at the expense of Berenyi. Strawberry hit his thirteenth home run and stole three bases, but when he came up with the bases loaded in the eighth inning and a chance to put us back in it, he struck out.

I was really looking forward to going against the Reds the next day because their pitcher would be Jay Tibbs, who was an old friend and teammate. We had pitched together for Lynchburg last year before he got traded, and this was the first time I'd be playing against anybody I had played with there. We had actually shared a glove at Lynchburg. The glove I had been using, I tried to put pine tar and stuff on it to dye it black, but it didn't come out too well and was kind of heavy. The only other glove I had was brand new and not broken in. So I tried Jay's glove one day, and I think I had a one-hitter and 16 strikeouts. I told him I had to go on pitching with that glove, so we just swapped back and forth.

We talked the day before about pitching against each other, and maybe swapping gloves again, but mainly we talked about hitting. I told him I was going to get a hit, and he told me that when he was at bat I should just lay it in there and let him connect with it. As it turned out, I didn't get a hit off him, and he struck out twice against me.

It turned out to be a great game and a real pitchers' duel. I had above-average stuff, as good as I'd had all year, and I was striking people out. The most satisfying strikeout for me came in the eighth inning. The score was 2–2, and they had runners on second and third with two outs and Dan Driessen up. Earlier in the season I had said that either Darrell Porter of the Cards or Mel Hall of the Cubs was my toughest out. But as the season went on, it was Driessen. He was hitting me every time I faced him with Cincinnati and later with Montreal. And in this game he was hitting me. I was nervous facing him in that situation. If I made the wrong pitch they would score some runs, and as late in the game as it was, that could be it.

I was really concentrating on him. I threw a fastball; he swung and missed. Then a curve for a ball. Then a fastball; he missed again. Then a fastball for a ball. Then I threw a curve way out of the strike zone. It was 3–2. Fitzgerald called fastball, but I shook him off. I figured since I had just thrown a curveball way outside, Driessen probably thought I wouldn't have the guts to come back with a 3–2 curve, because I was only a rookie.

So I threw the curve, and he was thinking fastball all the way because he was already out there committed to jump on the fastball, and the curve tied him up and he took it for strike three.

I pitched nine full, and Tibbs pitched eight, so we were both out of there when Hernandez hit a sacrifice fly in the eleventh to score Backman and get us the win, 3–2.

We beat the Reds twice more, 2–1 for Sid Fernandez's

second win, and 7–6 on Strawberry's fifteenth homer in the eighth. We came home and beat the Cards 4–3 in 12 innings and 9–8 in 10 innings. The fans were coming out and packing the stadium. We were thinking pennant. We felt it was about time for the Mets to go to the play-offs again.

We had one more game with the Cardinals before the Cubs came in. Davey decided to switch the pitching rotation. It was supposed to be my turn now; then Sid Fernandez was scheduled for the first game against the Cubs. But since Fernandez had only recently come up, Davey said he didn't want to put him out against the Cubs in front of 50,000 people in Shea Stadium. So he sent Fernandez against the Cards and held me back for the Cubs.

Fernandez said he had never pitched with just three days' rest before, and his arm started tightening up during the game. But we got all the hits we needed, including Strawberry's sixteenth home run with two men on, and won 9–3 for a sweep of the series and our sixth win in a row.

When the Cubs came in, we were on top of them by three and a half games, which was our biggest lead up to then.

The crowd started right off hollering for a strikeout when I threw my first pitch to Bob Dernier. Pitching with a couple of days extra rest left me extra strong. The ball felt light and it was coming harder than usual, but I didn't have much control. I got the count to 3–2, then I walked him. Dernier stole second, went to third on a groundout, and scored on a single.

I got two strikes on Leon Durham, and the crowd was right back in it yelling for a strikeout. Earlier in the season I used to try to shut that out of my mind. But now I liked it, for two reasons: it kept me pumped up, and I think it affected the hitters. When the crowd is yelling for a strikeout, I think the hitters may start thinking that I'm going to rear back and give them a fastball with something extra. Then I can get them on the curveball or make them swing at a fastball out of the strike zone. I struck out Durham and then Keith Moreland.

We got the go-ahead run in the seventh, and I was still pitching hard. The crowd had the wave going. I liked the wave except for when it got behind home plate, because you go into your windup and then suddenly you see a whole lot of hands go up in front of you and it can distract you.

I pitched through the eighth. I walked seven, which was the most I walked all year. But I struck out eight, gave up only four hits, and I think only about five balls were hit out of the infield. We beat the Cubs 2–1 to go up by four and a half. I felt so great after getting that win that I told the press it meant more to me than pitching in the All-Star game. I didn't quite mean that, but at the time that's how good I felt.

But things turned around for us just as quickly the other way. The Cubs took us the next three. Then we went on the road and the Cardinals took the first two. Suddenly we weren't getting any hitting or any pitching. Davey got thrown out of a couple games for arguing balls and strikes, because things were going so bad. Hernandez was in a slump, Strawberry was in a slump. Doug Sisk came up with a sore shoulder, and so did Mookie Wilson.

After five straight losses we were up only half a game over the Cubs, and Davey called a team meeting. He closed the door and kept the press out. He was pretty mad, because it seemed as if everybody had just gotten tired and gotten into an attitude where we didn't care. He didn't really chew out anybody in particular, but he asked us if anybody was too tired to play good baseball and if anybody wanted to go home. He said we were too good a team to fall apart now. After Davey, Rusty Staub talked to us. He said this was not going to get us down, and we were going to straighten out and be ready tomorrow. I agreed with everything they said, and I figured the meeting helped.

But it didn't help the next day, when I went against the Cardinals and Joaquin Andujar. I felt okay while I was warming up in the bullpen. But it was really hot. As a rule I figure I'm ready when I'm sweating, which is usually after 15 minutes of warm-up. But I started sweating much sooner in the heat, and so I probably didn't warm up enough. Anyway, I was tight when I started out.

Everything I threw, they hit—not too hard, but the balls had eyes. Every ball they hit was just out of somebody's reach. They got five singles, plus I threw my first wild pitch of the year. And I even hit Darrell Porter on the back of his leg with a curveball. You know things aren't going right when you hit a batter with an *off-speed* pitch. They got five runs in the first inning.

Then in the fourth I gave up three more runs without getting anybody out, and Davey brought in Tom Gorman for me. I had pitched 3 full innings and given up 10 hits and 7 runs. And the Cards stole five bases off me.

Things didn't get a whole lot better with me out of there. They ended up beating us 11–2. They got 17 hits off me, Gorman, and Brent Gaff, which was the most hits we gave up all year, and we had lost 6 straight games for the first time. Meanwhile, the Cubs were beating the Phillies, so we fell into second place. We had gone from four and a half up to half a game down in a week. After the game, Davey said, "This is rock-bottom."

The next day, Andujar was quoted in the newspaper as saying I was a good pitcher, but I would be better when I learned to throw a good change-up. He was right about that. I had been working on the change-up, but I hadn't been comfortable with the grip, so I was learning a new grip. I wanted to hold it sort of choked back in my palm, with the index finger and thumb together, and throw it with the same motion as the fastball. But it should come about 20 miles per hour slower, like 74 or 75, just enough slower so the batter doesn't have time to read-just. I had been having trouble with it all season. That day against the Cardinals, my curveball wasn't working, so they were just sitting on the fastball. And I couldn't throw my change-up for a strike if my life depended on it.

But I told myself this was just one bad day for me, and I'd come back against the Cubs when we went to Chicago the following week. Meanwhile we had to go into Pittsburgh and try to get back on the right track. At least in Pittsburgh they generally had very small crowds, almost like playing in a minor league park, and the way we were playing, we would feel right at home.

In the first game, we went up 3–0 against the Pirates, but they came back to beat us 6–4 for our seventh straight loss. The way we had turned from good to bad was unbelievable. Davey said, "In all my years in baseball, I've never seen anything like this."

Before the next game, Foster suggested to Davey that we have a team meeting, just the players, and Davey said okay. Foster, Staub, and Hernandez talked to us. They were pretty upbeat. They said this was only the beginning of August so we had plenty of time left in the season to get it back together, and we should believe in ourselves and just relax and go out and play the type of ball we were playing before.

We went out and beat the Pirates three straight. We went to Chicago trailing the Cubs by just half a game, and we would have four shots at the Cubs. I would pitch the first one.

At Wrigley Field, they throw stuff out of the stands at you, especially during batting practice, when you're out there shagging balls. I think they should have some security guards out in the center field bleachers where the "bleacher bums" sit. In most places, when somebody hits a ball into the stands, the fans will keep it. But there if somebody hits a ball into the stands during batting practice, you've got to watch your back because they may throw the ball at you. And on a ball hit to the fence, you've got to watch yourself when you go and get it, because they'll throw something down on you. It's pretty dangerous there; anything's liable to happen.

This time coming into Chicago, the Mets people warned us to be careful about our rooms and our phones because the Cubs fans had been encouraged by some radio broadcasts or something to aggravate us and not let us get any rest. The Cubs fans had apparently been told that in New York a lot of fans had called the rooms of the Cubs players and aggravated them, so now they were supposed to do it back to us.

When I got to my hotel room, I didn't tell the operator to stop the calls at first. So I got some calls. People calling me would say, "If you look out the window you're gonna get shot," or "If you come downstairs you're gonna get killed," or "When you pitch tomorrow, you better not turn your back to the stands." Stuff like that. It was silly. Either way you go when you pitch, you've got to turn your back to the stands. I just figured they were trying to intimidate me and get my mind off the game. That was the first time anything like that happened to me.

I thought about it a little, then I called down and told the operator to cut the phone off. A little while later, the message light went on. I called down to the operator and she said some guy named John said he'd meet me in the lobby. A while later the light came on again, and that message was that somebody named Terry would meet me at the bus tomorrow, he wanted to see me about something. Just different names every time. So I stopped taking the messages.

The next day, the Cubs got to me early. Again it was hot, and I warmed up too quickly, the way I had in St. Louis; I was sweating pretty good, but I wasn't loose. I got two outs, but I gave up a couple of singles and a walk, and then Jody Davis doubled down the right field line, and they were ahead 2–0.

In the third, I struck out Matthews and Moreland, but Durham doubled and Jody Davis came up again. I had struck him out three times in New York. In Chicago, you have to be careful, especially if the wind's blowing the way it was that day. You throw a mistake pitch there, you can forget about it. And with that flat mound, you have to concentrate more.

I threw Davis two fastballs, and he wasn't even close to them, swinging late. He was just overmatched on those fastballs. Now Fitzgerald called for a curveball. Usually in that situation if I'm going good and a hitter's late on my fastball, there's no way I would throw a curveball, unless I put it down in the dirt or way out of the strike zone just to show it to him. But I wasn't going so good. When Fitzgerald put down curveball, I just went with it. I did Jody Davis a favor and he took advantage of it. I threw him a curveball that hung, and he crushed it for a home run.

Lots of times when I give up a home run, it's no big deal. I just want the umpire to throw me the ball so I can get going again as soon as possible. But giving up this one, on a mistake pitch, that's the kind that really hurt, when you know that what he hit out of the ballpark wasn't your best pitch.

Now we were down 4–0. I walked Ron Cey. Then Dave Owen, their rookie shortstop, really tagged a fastball and tripled to the wall in center field. It was 5–0. With a man on third, I could at least end the inning by getting the pitcher out, Dick Ruthven. But I threw him a fastball too low. It bounced in the dirt right in front of Fitzgerald and hit his glove and rolled away.

I ran in to cover the plate, because Owen was coming. Fitzgerald didn't see him heading for the plate, and he tossed the ball to me easy instead of firing it. Owen slid and took my legs out. It was 6–0. Davey brought in Brent Gaff from the bullpen.

I don't swear much, but for the first time in the season I went into the dugout swearing and slammed down my glove. I was really mad. In my last 7 innings of pitching, against the Cards and the Cubs, I had given up 12 runs. Before that, everything had been pretty smooth. But now all of a sudden I thought things were catching up with me, and I could be in real trouble. Things I had gotten away with in the minor leagues I was not getting away with any more. It was rough for me right then, and for a little while I wasn't sure of anything.

Back in my hotel room later that night, I got a couple of calls. One guy said, "Jody Davis told me to tell you, thanks for the fat one." Another guy said, "If you hadn't lost that game, you'd be dead or your parents would be dead." Other players had told me they got threats too. It didn't bother me while I was in the ballpark. I just laughed about it. But in the room, I sat facing the door. The windows were locked anyway.

The next day, the Cubs beat us in a double-header. In the second game, Ed Lynch hit Keith Moreland with a pitch, and Moreland charged the mound. Everybody came out of both dugouts, and I went out just grabbing people and trying to help break it up. It wasn't that big a deal, mostly just holding and shoving, but the feelings between the clubs were not too good.

After the game, Strawberry and I had just finished eating and we were walking along the street when a bunch of guys pulled up in a car. They hollered out, "Hey, that's Strawberry and Gooden." It was four or five white guys, and they acted like they had been drinking. They asked us, "You guys looking for trouble?" We said no and just kept walking. They said, "Meet us at the corner and you'll get some trouble." They pulled up to the corner in front of us. A police car happened to come by and we flagged it down and told the police what was happening. They took care of it and we went on our way.

The next day the Cubs beat us again. In the seventh inning, when the Cubs were scoring a bunch of runs and had men on base, Walt Terrell hit Dernier in the helmet. This time the benches didn't empty, but the umpire threw Terrell out of the game, and Davey ran out to argue that the hit was not intentional. And there's no way it *was* intentional because with men in scoring position and Terrell ahead in the count he wasn't going to hit a guy, especially with a breaking ball, which is what the pitch was.

Fans started throwing beer down at us from over the dugout. Bill Robinson got beer thrown in his face, and he wanted to go up into the stands after the guy. Hubie Brooks and a couple of others almost went up, but some of us talked them out of it. We said it wouldn't be a good idea to go up into the stands, especially in Chicago.

Then in the ninth, Lee Smith, the Cubs pitcher, almost hit Foster in the head. Smith was ejected. I don't know if Smith really threw at him. But he was always pretty much right around the plate, and then this one pitch almost hits Foster. That gets you thinking.

But mostly what we were thinking about was that the Cubs had swept us four straight and we were behind them by four and a half games. We weren't in great spirits when we came home to play the Pirates. The team was pretty depressed. We were playing scared. Everybody was scared to go for the big play or take the extra base because they might make a mistake. We had us an attitude.

The Pirates beat us 11–0 for our worst loss of the year, and then again 4–1 for our sixth straight loss. Davey closed the clubhouse doors again to talk to us. But this time he wasn't mad, he was pretty positive. He told us there's no sense in folding now, that this kind of thing can happen, that we should just forget the past and take it from here.

I don't know what was going on with Strawberry. He was late showing up for the game, he got there during batting practice, and Davey benched him and I think fined him too. At that point Strawberry didn't like some things the press was saying, and he felt pressure from all the expectations people had for him. He wasn't doing all the things everybody thought he should be doing to help the team. Earlier one time in San Diego he had been late too, and Davey benched him then, but then he had pinch-hit and gotten the winning hit off Gossage. I didn't talk to him about the situation because he didn't bring it up. But I was glad that Hernandez was talking to him a lot, trying to get his head on straight. Hernandez was one of the best at that all season long.

Some people were saying that both Strawberry and I were doing poorly because we were feeling the pennant pressure. But I don't think that was the case for either of us. Strawberry wasn't really struggling at the plate that much, and it was just one of those things he would work out of. As for me, I don't think pennant pressure had anything to do with my last two bad starts. I just hadn't been able to get loose and get in rhythm. I had never had two games in a row where that happened, and after those Stottlemyre and I figured out what was wrong: because it was hot, I thought I was warmed up sooner than I was. Stottlemyre said I should start warming up five minutes more every time, change from 15 minutes to 20 minutes. And from there on I won seven games in a row.

But when I went against Pittsburgh I was feeling a little down, not only because of the way the team had been going but because I wasn't doing my job either. So this was a big game for the team and for me.

We got two runs in the first inning on a double by Brooks, and often when I get an early lead like that it's all I need. I get something to work with, which gives me more confidence. I felt strong because I hadn't pitched many innings lately. I struck out the first batter I faced and went on striking people out. I shut them out for 7 innings on 5 hits and got 10 strikeouts. And on the way I set my first record.

I wasn't aware of it until I happened to turn around and saw up on the Diamond Vision screen that the strikeout record for a Mets rookie pitcher was 178, which Jerry Koosman set in 1968, and I was approaching that. So with each strikeout the crowd was yelling louder and louder.

When I struck out Lee Mazzilli in the sixth inning I broke the record. They gave me a standing ovation. I stepped off the mound and waited. I didn't want to tip my hat or anything like that because that can seem like you're showing up the other team, and I didn't want to wake them up and get them pumped up to go after me. I just stepped back on the grass and looked around. I sort of wished they would stop so we could get on with the game, or that I had got the strikeout to end the inning. But the crowd stayed up there for two or three minutes, just kept clapping. At one point, it was feeling so good having the fans behind me and showing such appreciation that chills started going through my body, and I almost took my hat off. But I just waited. Then I went back up on the rubber and finally they stopped.

I pitched through the seventh and went out to pitch the eighth inning. But after I warmed up, they announced a pinch hitter, and Davey came to the mound to take me out. The crowd really got on him right away. I had thrown a lot of pitches, and Davey didn't want to take any chances. So I started off the mound and Davey stopped me. He said, "You ain't leaving without me, big boy." Because he knew that they would cheer me when I walked off, but then they would boo him something awful. So we waited there for Orosco to come in, then we walked to the dugout together. We were laughing all the way to the dugout because the crowd couldn't do anything but cheer while Davey was with me.

We beat the Pirates again, and then went to L.A., where we took two out of three from the Dodgers. Berenyi shut out the Dodgers in one game, and Sid Fernandez beat Valenzuela in the other. Fernandez was especially satisfied with that. It was the Dodger organization that had traded him away after he was the best pitcher in the Texas League last season, and he told me that Valenzuela was his idol.

We were two and a half behind Chicago and three and a half ahead of Philadelphia when we went up to Candlestick Park to play the San Francisco Giants four games.

It was my first time in there since the All-Star game. It was windy again, and kind of cold. For pitching, I thought that was great, because once you're warmed up you're fine and you don't get tired as quickly. I think it's worse for the hitters because they're always kind of cold and trembling, and they don't want the fastball in on their hands because if they get jammed and hit the ball near their cold hands they're really going to feel it.

I had a lot of confidence going into my twenty-fourth start, because I felt I was back in the groove from my last game, when I beat the Pirates. I struck out two Giants in the first inning, two in the second, one in the third, two in the fifth. I retired the first 10 hitters in a row and didn't give up a hit until Manny Trillo singled with one out in the fifth.

The Giants fans were hanging out "K" signs for me, black letters on orange paper, which are Giants' colors. Since the All-Star game, that had happened in a couple of other parks too, like Philadelphia and San Diego. That's a great feeling, when they do that for you on the road. It can't help the home team much to see that.

Meanwhile, Mike Krukow was throwing a great game also for the Giants and shutting us out. Our hitters said they could see his pitches, though, and eventually they would get him if I could just hold the Giants down until they did.

I pitched through nine, and with the score still 0–0 Davey pinch-hit for me. I didn't know how many pitches I had thrown. In the beginning of the season Davey would let me have around 105. Toward the middle he gave me 120 to 125. Now, if I was still throwing well, he might give me maybe 130 to 140 pitches. I thought I had one, maybe two, more innings in me, but Davey thought I'd thrown enough. Davey almost never let pitchers go extra innings.

And maybe he had the right idea, because the Giants let Krukow stay in, and in the tenth Wally Backman hit his first home run in two years to win it for us.

I had pitched 9 innings, faced 32 batters, given up 5 hits and 1 walk, and gotten 12 strikeouts and the win to make my record 11–8.

But still we couldn't quite get going. We lost two to the Giants on runs in the ninth before we won the last one. Then we dropped two to the Padres. We were five games behind the Cubs before my next start in San Diego.

CHAPTER 8

August 22–September 30

We needed to beat the Padres and they were tough. Not only had they beaten us the last two times we met, but they had been playing great ball the whole season and were leading the National League West by about 10 games. If I could beat the Padres we could at least break even on the road trip and go home feeling a little up. With the last week of August and most of September at home, maybe we had a shot at catching the Cubs.

I really had my good pitches working. I retired the first 11 Padres before Garvey doubled and Nettles hit a home run in the fourth. Even the pitch to Nettles I thought was a great pitch, but he was hot and had hit something like five home runs in his last five games. He tagged my fastball out of the park to put them up 2–0.

But we came back in the sixth with three runs to take the lead, and I was confident I could hold it because after Nettles I hadn't let anybody get on base and was striking batters out.

In the eighth I struck out Garry Templeton, and the umpire called time and stopped the game. I didn't know why. I looked in the dugout and I thought maybe something was wrong because Charlie Samuels, our equipment manager, was motioning out to the field with his hands. Stottlemyre and some of the players were yelling about something. Hernandez came over from first and I asked him what was going on, but he didn't know either. Finally Hubie Brooks ran over to the dugout to find out what was up. They told us.

When I struck out Templeton, that had been my 200th strikeout of the season. People in the stands didn't know because the scoreboard didn't have it up there. Samuels knew. He keeps up with different kinds of records. So he was calling for the ball for me, as a souvenir.

Then they flashed it on the scoreboard. It said I was only the eleventh major league pitcher to do that in his rookie year. A lot of fans stood up and clapped. Because it was San Diego, I thought maybe they would just clap a little, or maybe even boo, but they stood up and gave me a standing ovation.

We ended up winning 5–2. I pitched the whole game and gave up three hits. I didn't walk anybody, so I only pitched to 30 batters for the 27 outs. I struck out 9, to give me a total for the season of 202.

After the game, the press kept asking me how it felt to have 200 strikeouts. They said that no teenage rookie had ever finished the season leading the major leagues in strikeouts and that I was leading the majors now, and how did I feel about that? They said that the National League record for strikeouts in a rookie season was 227, set by Grover Cleveland Alexander in 1911, and that because I was averaging more than 10 strikeouts for every 9 innings, I had a shot at that record and even at the major league rookie record of 245 set by Herb Score in 1955—and how did I feel about all that? They asked me if I was thinking about breaking all those records and how it was going to affect me the rest of the season.

I told them I hadn't really been aware of the records,

and it would be fine if I could have the National League record and I would like to get it, but basically I just wanted to get the wins and help the team out. Whether you have strikeouts or not, it's much better to pitch for a winning team.

Before this past season, all I had known was who the top big league pitchers were. But I didn't know their records at all. I didn't know a single pitcher's won–lost record in the big leagues. I just knew who was good, not who the 20-game winners were and stuff like that. I didn't know who the last 30-game winner was. I knew that Nolan Ryan was the strikeout king of the major leagues, but I didn't know how many strikeouts he had. And I didn't even know who Grover Cleveland Alexander was.

When I first started pitching with the Mets, I didn't know anything about any of these strikeout records for a rookie or most strikeouts in a game or anything. I was just going for the wins. But now I started thinking about it a little bit, since I was so close. I figured it out one night: I had had 25 starts so far, and I would have maybe 5 or 6 more. All I needed was about five or six strikeouts a game, and I could get the National League record for a rookie.

But I didn't want to change my game plan and go for the strikeouts and end up getting a loss, because I'd rather have the wins than the strikeouts, and it was the wins that helped the team, not strikeouts. When we went home for the last week of August, we were four games behind the Cubs. So we still had a shot at first place, if we could pull pitching and hitting together at once.

It was going to be a tough home stand, especially for the pitching staff, because we had three double-headers in the first eight days.

The Giants came in and beat us in a double-header

and then a single game before we finally won the last game of the series. The crowd got into it and they booed some. I guess they figured that the Mets had folded. Some held up signs saying SAME OLD METS. But then there were some fans who stayed behind us whether we were winning or losing. Anyway, the fans didn't bother the team much, the players didn't get caught up too much in that. But it hurt to lose, especially to the Giants, who were last in their division. The Giants were one of the teams we had the most trouble with this year, along with the Cubs, and I couldn't understand it.

The Dodgers came in. I'd be going against Valenzuela again, and I felt a little pressure, worrying about the Cubs. But I kept telling myself that when I'm pitching, I can't be worrying about the Cubs or anything else, just take a hitter at a time, an inning at a time, and a game at a time. Hopefully, we could get some help from some other teams so we could catch the Cubs, but nobody was beating the Cubs much.

We had a big crowd. I gave up three hits and a walk in the first four innings against the Dodgers, but then I toughened up. We got three runs off Valenzuela in the fourth and took it from there. The only run I gave up was a home run to Mike Scioscia in the seventh. The fans got into the strikeouts. I struck out Dave Anderson four times. But the one the crowd liked most was when I got Guerrero in the eighth. He was getting on the umpire the whole time about the calls. I got two strikes on him with fastballs, then I threw him three curveballs in a row—two for balls and the third he took for strike three.

We won it 5–1. I got my second win over Valenzuela, my fourth straight win, and my second straight complete game. I gave up 5 hits and struck out 12.

The Mets' front office got Ray Knight from Houston to give us some more right-handed hitting power; he went in at third and Hubie was moved to short, so Hubie had to learn a new position. And they brought up pitcher Calvin Schiraldi from the minors. I had played with Schiraldi the year before in Lynchburg, and he had great stuff. So we hoped these two guys could help us down the stretch.

We beat the Dodgers twice more, and then the Padres came in for two double-headers in a row. We split the first one of those. But the Cubs just kept on winning, and we couldn't gain any ground.

The morning of the second Padres double-header, when I was supposed to pitch, I woke up with a headache, feeling weak. I was starting to get a cold or the flu or something. It wasn't bad enough to keep me out of the game, though. In fact, knowing I was weak just made me concentrate more to compensate for it. It was lucky we got some hits and runs that day. In the second inning, they got the bases loaded with two out and I managed to strike out the pitcher, Andy Hawkins. In the third they got a couple of runs before I pulled myself together. I walked Ed Wiggins, Tony Gwynn got a base hit, then they pulled off a successful double steal and had men on second and third. Garvey singled right by me up the middle to score them both. Then I struck out Graig Nettles, Terry Kennedy, and Kevin McReynolds on 10 pitches. That was the first time I ever struck out the side on just 10 pitches.

I pitched 8 innings and struck out 10, and we won 7–4. We won the second game too, 10–6. Strawberry hit home runs in both games, and it was good to think that maybe he was coming out of his slump, because we needed his bat.

We lost the last game of the series to the Padres, then went to St. Louis and lost two to the Cards. It seemed like every time we started getting things together and winning, we turned right around and began losing again.

In Pittsburgh, we took the first game from the Pirates, and I was supposed to pitch the second. But after the Pirates series, we were going home for three crucial games with the Cubs, and Davey switched the pitching rotation again. He put Schiraldi in for his first start against the Pirates so I could go against the Cubs. Schiraldi did his job, only gave up five hits, but we didn't get any runs for him, and the Pirates beat us 2–0.

The Cubs were now leading us by seven games. And they had beaten us seven straight times. We had about 20 games left in the season, but 6 of those were against the Cubs. I figured if the Cubs could beat us seven straight, it was possible for us to beat them six. Some of the players were talking about how in 1969 the Cubs were ahead of the Mets late in the season, and the Cubs failed and the Mets went on to win it all. We had that in mind. So we were going to take it a game at a time, and the first game was mine.

We had a great crowd, which they announced at more than 46,000. Also we heard that the National League President Chub Feeney was there, and the guy who was about to become the new Baseball Commissioner, Peter Ueberroth.

With an extra day of rest, I was really strong and up. The Cubs had been the last team to beat me back in Chicago a month before in that 9–3 game. So I was ready to get back at them for that.

I walked Bob Dernier to open the game, and he stole second, but then I retired the next 12 Cubs, including 7 by strikeouts. I was throwing mostly fastballs, and they just couldn't catch up with them.

The big one came in the second inning. I struck out Ron Cey, and they stopped the game. They announced that I had just set the National League rookie record with 228 strikeouts. The crowd stood up and clapped, and I just stepped off the mound and waited again. I knew going into that game that all I needed was a couple of strikeouts and I figured I'd get them early. I wanted to hurry up and get that out of the way so I could concentrate more on the game and not worry about strikeouts or records.

Meanwhile, we were getting seven runs in the early innings and knocking Dick Ruthven out of the game. Foster and Strawberry hit home runs, which was the first time this year they had both hit one in the same game.

I had that big cushion, but this time I didn't lie back on it the way I had before. I kept going right at them.

Way back at the beginning of the season, before my first start, players had suggested to me that hard as I throw, if I just let the first pitch go and be wild with it, it would intimidate the hitters, because they wouldn't know if the next one would be right at their head or what. But I never could do that. It did happen once, but I didn't mean to do it. In this game against the Cubs, I got two strikes on Leon Durham and I decided to really rear back and air one out to throw it by him. The pitch went by him, all right. It went by everybody and almost went over the screen. Durham grounded out, and when he was trotting back by the mound, he said, "What was that one? You working on a new pitch?"

In the fifth, Moreland hit a slow chopper down the third base line. Ray Knight was playing off the bag, and he charged it and scooped it up, but he bobbled it a little getting it out of his glove and didn't make a throw. Moreland didn't have great speed, and it would have been a close play anyway, so Knight decided not to take a chance on throwing it away. I didn't know I had a no-hitter going, but the fans were booing the scoreboard, and I turned around and looked up at it and saw that they had given Moreland a hit, and that was the first hit.

I walked three more Cubs in the game, but nobody reached second base after Dernier stole it in the first inning. I only gave up that one infield hit. And that was a close call. I figure had that play been in the eighth or ninth inning instead of the fifth, and I still had a no-hitter going, they probably would have called it an error. I felt bad, I guess, coming that close and not getting it.

But we got the win, 10–0, to cut the Cubs' lead to six. I felt good also about getting the National League rookie strikeout record. Reporters told me that with the 11 strikeouts I had this game, I had struck out 10 or more hitters 13 times this season, which tied the Mets record set by Tom Seaver in 1971. Also, with 235 strikeouts, I was now just 10 away from the major league rookie record set by Herb Score.

I read the next day that Gary Matthews, the Cubs left fielder, said that if I ever learned to throw a good slider to go with my other pitches I'd be practically unhittable. Actually, I do have a slider, which Vance Lovelace showed me how to throw in high school. The year before, at Lynchburg, when things weren't going too well, I showed my pitching coach, John Cumberland, that I could throw a slider. He would let me use it four or five times a game in certain situations. But the Mets really didn't want me messing around with it because my arm's still pretty young and tender, and it might have an effect on it, because you have to give a slider more twist to the side. So I didn't throw a single one in a game this year, just from time to time messed with it on the side to see if I still had it working. In games I went with just fastball, curve, and change-up and got by pretty well. But I think later in my career it'll be good to come up with another pitch. Then I'll show the slider.

After that week when I beat the Padres and Cubs I was named the National League Player of the Week for the second time. Bruce Sutter of the Cards and I won it together.

But we had needed to sweep the Cubs and we didn't. Rick Sutcliffe, who looked like he might be on his way to the Cy Young Award with a record of 14–1, shut us out the next day. Darling beat the Cubs the day after that, but we were still six back.

The Cards beat us twice, and we were seven games back. Then the Pirates came in for my twenty-ninth start.

The crowds really dropped off after the Cubs series. I guess they figured the race was over. There were only about 13,000 for my game against the Pirates, but we were still going to give it our best, and I still had my job to do. I was thinking a little bit more about strikeouts now, because I figured I might get the major league record in the next couple of starts.

When I'm pitching, I usually don't know how many strikeouts I've got; I find out after the game. But against the Pirates, I knew I was getting close because I was getting a lot of strikeouts early and I was sort of trying to keep up with how many I had.

We got two runs in the fourth on a home run by Hubie Brooks to lead 2–0. Other than that, John Tudor was pitching us pretty tough. With one out in the sixth, Marvell Wynne was up, and I figured I needed two more strikeouts for the record. The count was 2–2, and I got him to swing at a high fastball for the strikeout.

Then everything broke loose. Everybody in the stands stood up and cheered and yelled. I knew what had happened—I had miscounted. I stepped off the mound and looked at the scoreboard screen, which showed I had broken the major league rookie record with my 246th strikeout. And they showed Herb Score on the screen saying he congratulated me and wished me success in the years to come. All the players in the infield came over to shake my hand. Then I just stood there and waited. Again I didn't want to take off my hat because it was the middle of the inning. It went on for about three minutes. I just stood there and watched everything and felt pretty good.

Finally I went back to the rubber. And then I struck out Lee Lacy to end the inning.

That set off the crowd again. They gave me a standing ovation all the way to the dugout. When I was in the dugout, the crowd kept yelling, and the players were saying I should go back out there, so I went back out of the dugout and then I took off my hat. Usually it's the home run hitters they call back out of the dugout. That was the first time it had happened to me. I tipped my hat to the crowd and felt a little embarrassed and uncomfortable. But I also felt like I was on top of the world, with people showing how much they appreciated me like that. I felt like a big hero.

I ended up winning the game 2–0, with 16 strikeouts, 5 hits, and no walks.

After the game I looked at the charts and I thought maybe the charts were wrong because they showed I had done something I never did before in my life: I pitched a game without ever having three balls in the count to any batter. That was unbelievable. That whole game was unbelievable. The Mets put out a paper that showed my accomplishments that day and so far during the season. Besides the major league rookie strikeout record, it showed:

I had tied California's Mike Witt for the major league single game strikeout high this year.

I had my fourteenth double-figure strikeout game, breaking Tom Seaver's club record.

I had set a Met record for most strikeouts in a game by a rookie.

I had the biggest strikeout game for a Met since Seaver struck out 16 in 1974.

I was the first Met to pitch two shutouts in a row since Pat Zachry in 1980.

With my third shutout, I was the first Met rookie to have more than two since Jon Matlack had four in 1972.

I was the first major leaguer to strike out 16 batters in a complete game without giving up a walk since California's Frank Tanana in 1975.

By striking out the side in the fifth and eighth innings, I had struck out the side 14 times this year.

It was all just totally unbelievable.

The next day when I came into the locker room to dress for the game, one of the clubhouse guys brought over a stocking full of baseballs for me to sign. He said that Chuck Tanner, the Pirates' manager, and his coaches wanted me to autograph the balls for them. I felt like that was a big compliment. Another big compliment was what their pitcher, John Tudor, said about me in the papers the next morning. He said, "I would just like to throw one pitch like that in my life. Just to see what it feels like."

We were seven games behind the Cubs, but still I thought the fans would come out in appreciation for what we had done to be in second place after finishing last the year before. But the next day's crowd was about 6,000, the smallest of the year. Maybe it was just as well, because we had a lousy game, made errors and screwed up and got whipped 14–4. What there was of a crowd booed, but at least there weren't too many to boo. None of the players said much about it. Mostly we just laughed at the fans trying to make us feel bad.

We left home and went out to Chicago for our last try

at the Cubs. Even though it was our final shot at making up enough ground to have a chance at the pennant, I wasn't going to pitch out there because Davey didn't want to take a chance on sending me out with three days' rest and maybe mess up my arm.

Sutcliffe beat us in the first one. Then we lost again to go nine and a half down, the farthest we had been out of first place. And the Cubs had beaten us all eight times so far in Chicago. Finally, Berenyi pitched a two-hitter and Strawberry hit his twenty-second home run and knocked in five runs, and we got our first win of the season in Wrigley Field, 9–3.

But we were eight and a half games out, and we were pretty realistic about that. What we wanted to do now was hold on to second place, and the Phillies were three games behind us when we went into Philadelphia for three games.

I was to pitch the first night in Philadelphia, and that day an article came out in a New York paper that had my agent saying he would be asking for a lot of money for my next year's contract. They mentioned how Valenzuela had held out during spring training his second year in 1982 until he got what he wanted, and that my agent figured I should probably get more now than Valenzuela got then, which was $350,000.

That was the first time it had come up in the papers, and it kind of interfered with me. I didn't want to get a bad rap with the Mets. The way it was put in the paper made it seem as though once I threw a couple numbers on the board I wanted more money—and I wasn't even thinking about it at that point. I never had anything to do with that. I was sorry it was brought up so early, because I didn't want any misunderstanding with the Mets officials or the players, especially with the season still going on. But nobody on the team said anything about it.

I came into the Phillies game hot and ready to go. The first hitter, Jeff Stone, singled and stole second. But then I struck out the side. I struck out two in the second and two in the third.

From then on it turned into one of those games in which I didn't walk anybody and didn't give up too many hits and got most of the outs by strikeouts, but everybody who got on base gave me trouble and it became a weird kind of game.

In the fourth with one out, Von Hayes singled. I tried to pick him off first and got called for a balk, putting him on second. Then he stole third. I struck out Mike Schmidt and ended the inning on a fly out.

In the fifth, Greg Gross singled and stole second; then I struck out the side.

With Shane Rawley pitching a fine game against us, it was 0–0 going into the sixth.

I started off the inning getting two strikes on Jeff Stone. I had great movement on my fastball that game, and now I wanted to go with a fastball that ran in on him. The pitch tailed in so much it almost hit him, but he swung and missed, and then the ball went off Fitzgerald's mitt and rolled to the backstop, and Stone got to first on the passed ball after the strikeout. Then he stole second again.

I went into my stretch and saw Hubie Brooks break for second behind Stone. I turned and threw for the pickoff. But Hubie had stopped. He was pretty new at shortstop and we had never worked on that pickoff play. He broke for the bag but when I threw he just stopped a few feet away. My throw went on into center field and Stone went to third.

I struck out Juan Samuel, but then Von Hayes singled to drive in Stone and we were down 1–0.

Foster tied it up right away with a home run in the

seventh, and I figured we were back in good shape because I could hold them the rest of the way and our hitters were starting to get at Rawley.

In the eighth, I struck out Al Oliver. Then I let down a little, and Rawley singled to center. With Stone up, I threw a wild pitch that bounced by Fitzgerald, and Rawley went to second. Then Stone beat one down onto the turf so it bounced high up in front of me. With his speed, when he hits a chopper like that on the artificial turf you can just forget about it. He beat it out, and Rawley went to third.

On my first pitch to Juan Samuel, Stone stole second. Hernandez came over and said to watch out for a bunt because I had already struck out Samuel twice, and with runners on second and third and one out, most likely he'd try to bunt for a hit or they'd try a squeeze to get the run in.

I said okay, but instead of pitching from a stretch, I started to go into a windup. Hernandez yelled, "Step off!" I stopped and stepped off the rubber because I knew that Hernandez was trying to get me to pitch from a stretch instead of a windup, so I could watch the man on third. But it was too late. I had just started to move my hand for the windup when I heard Hernandez and stopped and stepped off, and I hoped the umpire hadn't seen it. But it was a balk all the way, and the umpire called it. Hernandez accepted the blame for it, but I should have known enough to go ahead and make the pitch, once I had started. The balk brought in Rawley from third with the lead run, which I figured would likely be the winning run, with us just having one more at-bat against Rawley.

That was the final straw—base runners had really done me in that game. I walked off the mound to try to get myself together. They had stolen six bases off me, I had thrown a wild pitch and made an error on a pickoff throw and committed two balks, and the last one might cost us the ball game. All this time I had thrown great pitches and struck out a whole lot of batters. I tried to accept what had happened, and to realize that what was done was done, to relax and not worry about it. Samuel got back in the batter's box and was ready to hit. But I wasn't ready to pitch. I wouldn't step back on the mound until I had really gotten myself back together. The fans were booing me because I was taking so much time.

About three minutes after the balk had been called, I was ready, and I went back up onto the mound. I struck out Samuel. And then I struck out Von Hayes to end the inning strong.

We didn't score in the ninth so we lost 2–1. I had struck out 16 batters without any walks for the second straight game, and lost it on a balk in the eighth inning. After the game Steve Garland told me I had broken a couple of Sandy Koufax's records by striking out 16 hitters 2 games in a row and by striking out 41 in 3 consecutive 9-inning games. That was nice to know, but it was disappointing to make so many mistakes in a close game at such an important time.

The next day, Strawberry hit a three-run homer in the ninth to beat the Phillies. But then we had a game in which we just kind of fell apart in the field. Routine plays we couldn't make, bunts we didn't know what to do with. Even Hernandez, one of the best fielders in the game, let one ball go through his legs; on another one he fielded it and then threw over the head of the pitcher, who was covering first. I never saw anything like it all year, sort of like the Bad News Bears all over again. Five or six errors. The Phillies scored five runs off Ron Darling in the first inning, and going against Steve Carlton we could just about forget it right there. It was just a wild, long, strange day. We lost 13–5. We were only two games ahead of the Phillies for second place. The Cubs were losing, but we were still eight games behind them, and their magic number was down to three.

Davey said that youth and inexperience cost us in September, but I didn't think that was it. I thought it was more that we just hit a slump during that period, and it seemed like the Cubs never went into a slump the whole season except right at that time, when they were losing five straight. But we were losing also, so it didn't matter much.

We went back to Shea for our last home stand against the Expos and the Phillies. I was going against the Expos in the Sunday game, and the Mets flew in my parents to see it. I had been feeling weak from a head cold for the last couple of days, but I wanted to pitch this game anyway. We were still worried about holding second place. Another worry I had was that this was a day game, and I hadn't won a day game all year. So I had to make a special effort to concentrate really hard.

Right away I could tell I didn't have my good fastball. Feeling the way I did, I just didn't have the usual steam behind it. I got two outs in the first inning, then Andre Dawson singled. I figured he'd be running on me. I caught him leaning and picked him off first base. I had been working on the side all year trying to improve my move, and this day I was really concentrating on doing everything right. The first thing I did right was make a clean move off the rubber and pick off Dawson.

It probably helped us that the Expos went with a rookie pitcher, Joe Hesketh, who hadn't pitched many games. We got a couple of runs in the first inning to give me a cushion to work with.

In the second inning, I got one out, then Gary Carter and Dan Driessen singled. But I was able to strike out

Roy Johnson and Tim Wallach. In the fourth, Dawson led off with a double, went to third on a fly ball, and scored on a groundout. Our lead was cut to 2–1. In the fifth I walked my first batter since my game against the Cubs four starts ago. But I managed to get the side out.

It was already a real tough game for me. By the sixth inning I really should have come out, but I wanted to pitch some more because we had the lead and I wanted to hold it for us if I could. Steve Garland gave me some vitamins to take and an inhaler to help clear my head up.

I hung in, just moving the ball around and mixing up my off-speed pitches, because my fastball was slow. In the sixth, Dawson got a single, his third straight hit. I struck out Gary Carter, and Dawson tried to steal on the pitch and Fitzgerald threw him out—only the second or third time all year we got somebody trying to steal off me.

In the bottom of the sixth we scored two runs, and got another in the seventh. I hit two singles and scored a run.

I got them out in the seventh and eighth, and then I couldn't go any more. I told Davey I was feeling too weak to pitch. A couple of guys were telling me I had 9 strike-outs, just needed one more to get 10, and I had struck out 10 or more for the last 5 games in a row. So I had nine after eight innings, but there was no way I could have gone back out there.

We won 6–1 to make my record 17–9. Meanwhile the Cubs were sweeping a double-header to clinch first place. The Cards had moved into third, but we were ahead of them by four and a half.

The Phillies came in for three games to close out our last home stand before going up to Montreal to wrap up the season there. We beat the Phillies the first game to clinch at least a tie for second place. We beat them again to nail down second. There was a very small crowd for that one, but we were happy not only because we had second place but because Rusty Staub won the game for us with a two-run pinch-hit homer in the ninth. It was his first home run that year. But that home run put Staub in the record books with Ty Cobb. Staub was forty-one, and they told us that now he and Ty Cobb were the only players in the history of baseball to hit a home run before they turned twenty and after they turned forty. We were happy for Rusty, and some of the guys were teasing him that that home run might have given him another year on his contract too.

We didn't have any celebration for finishing in second place, no champagne or anything, but we felt real good. After finishing last or next to last for so many years, we felt pretty satisfied with second place. Even the young players like myself could feel that way because we all knew where the Mets had come from and what the expectations had been at the start of the season, and we had done a lot better than that.

We beat the Phillies for the third straight time in the final game at Shea. Davey decided to have me pass up my last scheduled start in Montreal. He said I had nothing more to prove, and he figured I might as well save my arm. I had already pitched 218 innings, which was the most I had pitched in my career.

It didn't bother me not to pitch that last start. If we still had a chance for the pennant I would have wanted to pitch. But we had already clinched second and that was going to be it no matter what happened. The only thing within reach for me was that, with my 276 strikeouts, I was only 13 short of Tom Seaver's all-time Met record for a season. A record like that would be great to have, but I didn't think too much about it. I usually try not to get caught up too much in individual stats. It wasn't worth taking a chance by trying to get it. And the possibility of getting 13 strikeouts in that one game was pretty slim, especially since I still had that head cold that had bothered me so much that I hadn't been able to come back and pitch the ninth inning against Montreal at Shea. So I figured that one last start wasn't going to make much difference. I agreed with the move Davey made to let me sit it out and let Calvin Schiraldi get another start.

Some of the players got on me about it. They said I was ducking my last start to protect my batting average. In that last game I pitched, I got 2 hits, which gave me 14 hits in 70 at-bats. I hit .200 for the season right on the button. Mookie Wilson owed me a dinner.

The Expos beat us 7–0. Then we beat them 8–4. Finally they beat us 5–4 to end the season. In those last two games, Strawberry hit 3 home runs, so he ended up with 26 homers and 97 RBI's, which was the best on the team in both departments. I felt good about that. Lots of people had been saying that Strawberry had a bad year after being Rookie of the Year the season before. But he actually had a better year than his first one. It wasn't a bad year, not at all, not for him *or* me.

CHAPTER 9

September 30—

Usually in Montreal we either had a lot of time after a game or we had to rush to the airport, because we flew commercial up there and they had to book a flight ahead of time and of course we never knew exactly when we'd be finished. This time we had about two and a half hours before the bus left for the airport, so we just hung around in the clubhouse talking to each other, drinking beer, congratulating each other on the great season we had had.

Davey made a speech. A couple of veteran players like Foster and Staub made speeches, and anybody else who wanted to spoke. Everybody was saying they enjoyed playing with everybody else on the team, and they hoped we could have a winning season next year and go to the play-offs, and they hoped everybody had a great off-season and stayed in shape and kept out of trouble and would be ready to come to spring training.

Some flew directly home from Montreal, but the majority flew back to New York together. The mood on the plane was very up. There was a lot of horseplay and joking around. It had been a long season, and everybody was ready to go home. I was happy to be going home to

see my family, because I hadn't been home for six
months, not since the last day of spring training on April
1, when I made the team. But then again I was kind of
wishing the season could have gone on a little longer
because toward the end I picked up and was going really
well consistently. Now all of a sudden it was September
30 and the season was over.

Once we got to the airport in New York and were
waiting for our luggage, I guess everybody realized we
wouldn't be seeing each other for a long time, and maybe
some we wouldn't be seeing again at all. It crossed my
mind that maybe not everybody would be back with the
club next year, because that's the way it is in baseball.
The mood kind of changed there, when we were starting
to split up.

Some of the players said if they didn't come back next
year they wanted to wish the team good luck. Ed Lynch
and I talked a lot while we were waiting. We had become
pretty close. He had started off the year real well, but the
season didn't turn out to be all that great for him. He said
he'd probably be out of there by next year. He lived in
Miami, and we said we'd keep in touch and maybe get
together in the off-season.

Players got their luggage and we went to the clubhouse at Shea Stadium and got the rest of our stuff out of
our lockers and hung around awhile. I had moved out of
my apartment before we went up to Montreal, so that
night I stayed at a hotel. I had a flight home the next
morning, Monday morning.

It was the first time in a long time that I'd been on an
airplane without the team. So I felt like I was by myself,
because there was nobody to talk to or joke with. I was
really excited about going home. It seemed like it took
forever. I kept trying to fall asleep to make the time go,
but every time I did I'd wake right up because I was

thinking about things. I was wondering how things would be when I got home, how my friends were going to react, everything. Just the idea of seeing Florida again and thinking about all that made it seem like forever for the plane to get there.

When I got off the plane I saw my family waiting there. It was great to see them and know I was home. A reporter for Channel 8 was there too, and he wanted to interview me. He asked me how it felt to be back home after a great season, and if I would change now that I was kind of a celebrity. I told him that I felt it had been a successful season for me and the Mets, and that I was looking forward to seeing everybody. And while maybe some things around me might change, I didn't see where I was going to be any different. I was just six months older and I knew something about pitching in the big leagues. But mainly it just felt great to be back in Tampa.

When we got home, they had signs hanging up in the neighborhood: WELCOME HOME, DR. K, WELCOME HOME, DWIGHT, GLAD TO HAVE YOU HOME. Everybody came to the house, neighbors, friends I hadn't seen in a long time, a whole lot of people. They had music on, and there was lots of food, and there were lots of hugs and kisses. I felt so great with all those people around showing appreciation. Actually I had been tired when I got home at about three-thirty in the afternoon, but I was having such a good time that I forgot about it. The party went on until about twelve that night. I was on my feet the whole while, talking, laughing with everybody, answering questions about how things were in the big leagues, finding out what had been going on with everybody there. It was just a great time.

One of the first things I did was to pick up my Mercedes 380 SE that I had ordered earlier. Then my parents and I went looking for a new house. I wanted to buy a bigger home for my parents, and we found a nice four-bedroom house with a fenced-in backyard in a quiet neighborhood not too far away from where we were living. I would be living in the new house too when I was in Tampa, at least for the time being.

Things were pretty different for me in Tampa. Last year nobody ever came up and said, "Are you Dwight Gooden?" or anything like that. Never. But now, when I went places, even if it was just down to a store, somebody might say, "Are you Dwight Gooden?" Or they might come up and say, "Let me shake your hand for a great season." Then some others nearby might hear that, and they would look, and they would want to come over and get an autograph. Before you knew it, you had an autograph session going on. That happened a lot.

Lots of times I've pulled into a gas station to get some gas, and somebody in another car would happen to look at me and would say, "You're not Dwight Gooden, are you?" Sometimes I might be wanting to say no, but I would go ahead and say yeah. Then they would get out and come over to shake my hand. Then they might say, "Wait a minute, I want your autograph." Then it would take them about five minutes to find a pen. I never said, "No, I'm not Dwight Gooden." But there've been times I wanted to say it, like when I'm in a hurry or just don't feel like talking. I just think it's nicer to give people a few minutes of your time when they are trying to show appreciation.

The phone rang all the time. When I got home I told my parents I thought it would be best to get the number changed. We got an unlisted number, but it was still the same, if not worse. Everybody got the number anyway. It was amazing. Friends called a lot, of course, and teammates from the Mets. There were always calls from newspaper reporters and radio and TV people. Lots of females called, ones I didn't even know. I didn't know how they got the number either. They called and said things like, "I know you don't remember me, but I've been watching you all year, and maybe we could get together." Lots of calls like that. They might say they met me someplace, and maybe they did, but I didn't remember, and I just told them I was pretty much tied up.

I mean, the phone rang at all times of the night. It got to be just ridiculous. My parents were enjoying everything about what was happening with me except the phone ringing late at night. Sometimes if I was out in the evening and there were a lot of phone calls, my parents would say, "Why aren't you home, with all these people calling for you?" And I'd say, "Well, I don't know when they're gonna call." But I think my parents pretty much enjoyed all the attention. And they hadn't changed either. They still spent time with their same friends and everything, just like I did. What I figured I'd do was, when we moved into the new house, we'd have two numbers so mine would be different from theirs.

A couple of agents still called from time to time, wanting to check out my availability, but not as many as before. A few people called about making appearances, but mainly they called Jim Neader or Jay Horwitz at the Mets, and I didn't do too many of those. A couple of schools called and wanted me to talk to their classes. One was the elementary school where I had gone. They wanted me to talk to the sixth grade, and I thought I might do something like that where I would be comfortable. But when high schools wanted me to talk to their classes, that made me feel a little strange. I was afraid that maybe not too many people there would pay attention to what I said because they might figure that since I was only two years older than some of them I probably didn't know much more than they did—not about life, anyway.

I had one call about modeling. I never thought anybody would call me for that. They wanted to know how I felt about doing some modeling for clothes, and I told them I didn't know, I never had any experience with anything like that. They said to get back to them if I was interested. I might give them a call some time and see what's going on.

There were a couple of things I did differently now. When I went out to the mall to do some shopping and look around, where last year I could just wear shorts and cut-off shirts, now I felt I should be a little more proper. Especially on weekends when there were a lot of people who would recognize me, maybe even some Little Leaguers who might idolize somebody like me, if they see you're dressed in just shorts and house shoes and a T-shirt, that's not so good. So I dress a little more respectably. That's just a rule of my own, and it's not too bad a price to pay.

Another thing that was different was playing basketball. I've had to make a little sacrifice there. It's crossed my mind a lot that I could have an accident with my arm or hand. During the off-season I used to look forward to playing basketball every day. Last year just about every night I used to go to the University of South Florida gym, where there were always lots of people waiting in line to play. And they played hard, running up and down the court and slam-dunking and everything. But now I just couldn't do that any more. Sundays my friends played some basketball, and I'd go out with them. We didn't play serious ball, just took it easy. But then a lot of people started coming around and wanted to get a serious game going, and some of them I hadn't seen before, guys with size who were really out to play all out. And maybe there'd be a little challenge situation also where they wanted to show me how tough they were and how well they could play. I wanted to play, but then I'd start thinking: These guys here are kind of crazy and they're going to be out there bumping and rebounding hard and all that, and it's easy to get your hand caught in the rim, or trip and fall and jam your fingers.

So with neighbors and friends, I'd play. But when others came around, I just got a ball and went down to another hoop and played around by myself. Much as I wanted to play good, hard basketball, I couldn't afford to get caught up in anything where I could get an injury.

Other than that, the only worry I had was that somebody might be jealous of me or something like that, and get into an attitude and try to draw me into it. I was talking to one of my friends, a girl, and she said that some guy told her he was going to get me somehow or other, maybe try to hurt me. Somebody I didn't even know. I asked her why. She said the guy just didn't like me for some reason. So far, I haven't heard any more about anything like that. I just have to watch my back now and then, I guess. But I haven't had any real problems of that type at all.

In October, I went over to the Instructional League at our complex in St. Pete for a few days and threw some pitches to work on a couple of things. I threw a lot of change-ups so I could get to where I could throw strikes with it consistently. And I worked on pitching out of the stretch, trying to make my move to the plate quicker so I wouldn't give up so many stolen bases. John Cumberland, the Lynchburg pitching coach, worked with me there, and he put a stopwatch on me, and he said that when I pitched out of the stretch I had cut down the time it took me to kick and throw from two seconds last year to 1.3 or 1.4 seconds now. He said that was a good time.

And also he said my change-up was coming along fine. He said that if I threw it next year like I was throwing it there, I could win 30 games next season. It was part of his job to help me get confidence, so I don't know if he really meant that exactly, about 30 games; maybe he was just trying to make me feel good. I was just glad to see I was getting better.

But my arm began to feel tired and heavy, so I figured I'd better stop pitching over there and let it rest a couple of months.

Around the middle of October they announced the Cy Young Award for the top pitcher in the National League, and I was real proud to finish second behind Rick Sutcliffe of the Cubs. My ERA was 2.60 to his 2.69, but while my record was 17–9, his was 16–1, which is just unbelievable. I was more than satisfied finishing second behind him in my rookie year. UPI named Sutcliffe and me to the UPI National League All-Star Team, which was another nice recognition to have.

Everybody was talking about how I would win National League Rookie of the Year, how I was a shoo-in for it and all that. I tried not to anticipate it too much, but when veteran players and the press and everybody is telling you that it's a foregone conclusion, it's hard not to expect to get it. A couple of weeks before they announced it, a Tampa radio broadcaster even had me make a comment about how great it was to be Rookie of the Year so he could have a tape of my reaction on hand when the time came.

On November 19, the Mets brought me up to New York to be there at Shea Stadium when they announced Rookie of the Year and to hold a press conference afterward. Mets officials and a lot of press and so on were in the Diamond Club at Shea Stadium waiting for the official word. We had food and talked while we waited. Jay Horwitz, the public relations director, told me that he already knew I had won it.

At about six o'clock, a TV guy said it was final, it had come across the wire that I was named National League Rookie of the Year. They said that I got 23 first-place votes out of the 24 members of the Baseball Writers Association of America who voted for the award. The other vote went to Juan Samuel of the Phillies.

All the writers and everybody congratulated me, and Mr. Doubleday also shook my hand. It was great that the Mets now had two Rookie of the Year winners in a row, Strawberry and me, and I was very proud and very happy to win it. I only wished that it could have been a little more of a surprise. But it was a great honor to have, especially because it's an award that you only get one shot at in your whole career.

Jim Neader and the Mets started talking about my contract for next year. Jim and I had discussed what I should get and what would be realistic, based on what other Rookies of the Year had gotten before, and what other pitchers got, and the year I had, and so on. Other than that I wanted to stay pretty much out of it.

I think I'm pretty clear in my head about the money thing. I plan to be using the same apartment in Port Washington that I did last year. And the money I was making last year and getting by on, I'll try to use about that same amount, and the rest of it I'll just put away. I won't be buying two or three cars or throwing money around. It won't be a problem. The main thing is you want to save as much as you can for later on. One day when you're out of baseball you don't want to have to come back and coach or get a regular job or anything like that. You just want to relax and enjoy what you've worked so many years for.

Marriage is not on my mind for the time being. I'm not ready for it. I wouldn't mind getting married and having a family, a couple of kids, maybe when I'm thirty or around there. Right now I just like being single and concentrating on pitching and becoming a better pitcher.

Next year my life off the field will probably be a little different. When I go around in New York more people will know who I am and they won't call me "Strawberry" or other names. I'll probably go out a bit more—I don't mean to clubs and that type of thing, I'll just try to see more. This year it was pretty much just staying home in my apartment or in a hotel on the road mostly being to myself and not seeing much. I want to look around in all the cities and see what there is to see.

If anything were to happen to me all of a sudden, like if my arm went out and I couldn't pitch any more the rest of my life, I can always go to school, because it's in my contract that I can go to college any time as long as I'm in the Mets' organization and they will pay for it. But beyond that, I haven't given it any thought. I'd probably get into some kind of business, but I don't know what. Baseball has been everything to me for about as long as I can remember. That's all I've dreamed, eaten, slept. I could go out and play ball every day, year round, if I had somebody to play with.

At least I know I'll be on a baseball card, because after your first full season they make a baseball card about you. I never was a big collector of them, unless I went into a store and saw Pete Rose on a card, or Mike Schmidt or Steve Garvey or somebody like that, then I might buy the pack of gum just because their picture was on it. But now I'll be on one because it's automatic, and they've already gotten a picture of me from the Mets to put on a card.

In November I took about a month off, just sat back and took it easy, relaxed, slept. I had thought maybe I'd go somewhere, maybe Walt Disney World in Orlando for a few days. I have never been there. I've never been out of the country except for Montreal, and I wouldn't mind seeing some places. I would like to see Puerto Rico, maybe even Japan, or Hawaii.

But I didn't do anything or go anywhere. I just relaxed and hung around. And in December I started back throwing easy so I'd be in real good shape for spring training in February. I had a lot of time to think about next season.

Strawberry had told me that the next season was going to be a lot tougher for me, people were going to be expecting me to do a lot more than I did in my first year. He said pitchers were pitching him a lot tougher now. They didn't mind walking him and they didn't give him anything good to hit, and it was tough to put numbers up on the board when nobody was really pitching to you and you had to swing at bad pitches just to get an at-bat. He said that next year the hitters were going to be taking a lot of my off-speed pitches and sitting back on the one pitch they wanted. But he said that if I got by my second year pretty well, everything else would probably fall into place for me.

It's true that the hitters didn't know me when I first came up, didn't know how I threw or what pitches I liked to go with in certain situations. I think that helped me out a lot. But then again, I hadn't faced those hitters either, so I didn't know what pitches they had trouble with until after a couple times around. All in all, though, next year I think hitters and teams will be after me more because of the numbers I put up my first season, so I figure it will be tougher next year.

I know that there is supposed to be a "sophomore jinx," and especially after a rookie season where you do really well the next year may be a bad year. That scares me because I don't think I could put up with a bad year—

like a losing record or a high ERA. I probably couldn't handle going to the ballpark every day and know that I'm not doing my job, not doing what I'm capable of doing, or that every time I take the hill I'm losing off my mistakes.

I've never experienced that, and I think it'd be pretty tough experiencing it the first time. But it wouldn't be a case where I would go out and start drinking or taking drugs or messing myself up. It would never affect me that way. I wouldn't quit. I'd just have to keep coming back and taking the whoopings, I guess, and trying to overcome it.

So I'll be working hard in spring training not only on my pitches but on going over notes and charts on hitters. I'll see what I did this year and what was successful in certain situations. And where I wasn't successful, I'll have to change strategy. I'll also keep some notes of my own on the toughest hitters, what pitches they take or swing at, how they react in various situations.

During the off-season, I also thought a lot about our prospects for next year as a team. I figured the Cubs were solid, but they couldn't last too much longer the way they were because they had a lot of older players—Cey, Bowa, Matthews. San Diego had a great season in the National League West, but I don't think their pitching is that tough. They just put so many runs on the board.

The Mets had a good team. I didn't think we really *needed* anything. Last year I thought there was just a little weakness in that we had a lot of young players, and a lot of players who hadn't played together too much and didn't know each other so well. This year we should come together better.

But I knew the Mets were out to get a catcher. I thought Fitzgerald did a good job last year. I had met him the year before, and he caught me when I pitched down in Tidewater in the Triple-A championship series, and he helped me out a lot then and this year. We got along real well together, on and off the field. But he was young also. This was his first full season with the Mets, and it is real tough catching a young pitching staff, with all that you have to know and all the responsibility you have to carry. And he hit in the .240s and only hit two home runs. So I thought that if we got another power hitter—an outfielder or a catcher—that could make a lot of difference.

Then they made the trade and got Gary Carter from the Expos. I couldn't believe it. A catcher *and* a power hitter all in one. And not just *any* catcher and power hitter, but just about the best in the game, or close to it. They had all his stats in the papers. Last year he hit .294 with 27 homers and tied Mike Schmidt for most RBI's in the National League with 106. He had won four Gold Gloves for his work behind the plate and had been the National League All-Star catcher for the last six years in a row.

Carter has been my dream of a catcher. I had been watching him on TV for so many years. And then when he caught me in the All-Star game, with all his experience, he just brought everything out of me that I had to give. Every pitch he made me work. He kept talking to me behind the plate, keeping my mind on the game, keeping my confidence up, making sure that I knew what I was doing with every pitch I threw. He had a winning attitude.

Plus his arm. My biggest problem by far last year was runners stealing bases off me. Now I would have Carter behind the plate with an arm to throw those runners out if I gave him half a chance. With him back there, I would be more relaxed, more comfortable, wouldn't have to feel rushed with men on base.

After the All-Star game, I thought a lot about what a dream it would be to have Gary Carter catching me every game. I never imagined the Mets would get him. I had no thoughts at all that they were even trying to get him. Now it had come true. The news that we would have Gary Carter going into next season instantly gave me a lot more confidence.

The first thing I said when the papers called me for a reaction to the trade was, the best thing about getting Carter was that I didn't have to face him as a hitter any more. But that was just a joke. The best thing about getting Carter was getting Carter.

Naturally we had to give up a lot in the trade. First of all, Hubie Brooks. Hubie kept us loose, kept us in a good mood, kept us up and going, and he will be missed by me and a lot of other players on the Mets. For Fitzgerald, I hope he has a good opportunity to play and develop up in Montreal, because he is a good catcher with a good attitude and he could go a long way.

And then Floyd Youmans. He and I have been friends for so long, high school teammates, and then picked one-two by the Mets in the 1982 draft. We had really looked forward to pitching together on the Mets some day soon. When the Mets traded away Walt Terrell earlier, I thought that might give Youmans a chance to come up to the Mets right away, the way I did. Then when he got traded to Montreal as part of the deal for Carter, I talked to him. I told him I thought it was a good break because they had to have big plans for him in Montreal, either to use him right away or maybe bring him up at the All-Star break. I expect there's a good chance I'll be pitching against Youmans this year when we play the Expos. That would be something for both of us.

Strawberry called me from his home in California. He said he couldn't believe the Carter trade. Just like me, he was sorry to see Hubie leave. But, he said, "We got just what we've always needed."

So just then it looked like everything was really going my way, more than I had ever expected, even more than I had thought at the end of my rookie season. I had a birthday in November, so I'm twenty years old and not a teenage pitcher any more. Next year I'll be more prepared physically and mentally than I was this year. I'll be trying a little harder, I'll have more confidence, and I think I should be more successful.

In any case, I'll just take it a game at a time and not let anything intimidate me or get me down. Sometimes I just can't wait to get out there and pitch again and see how it all turns out.

December 1984